National 4 & 5

Modern Studies

Democracy in Scotland and the UK

Frank Cooney
Gary Hughes
David Sheerin

HODDER
GIBSON
AN HACHETTE UK COMPANY

The Publishers would like to thank the following for permission to reproduce copyright material:

Photo credits p.4 © KeystoneUSA-ZUMA/Rex Features; p.6 ©Photodisc/Getty Images/ World Landmarks & Travel V60; p.8 © erolus - Fotolia.com; p.11 © Jonathan Swingler – Fotolia; p.13 © Chris Hepburn / iStockphoto; p.14 (both) © Frank Cooney; p.17 © Simon Chapman/LNP/Rex Features; p.19 © Anna Gowthorpe/PA Archive/Press Association Images; p.22 © Dave Thompson/PA Archive/Press Association Images; p.29 © David Cheskin/PA Archive/Press Association Images; p.31 PA/PA Archive/Press Association Images; p.32 © PA/ PA Wire/Press Association Images; p.33 © PA/PA Archive/Press Association Images; p.34 © Ben Curtis/PA Archive/Press Association Images; p.36 © Rui Vieira/PA Archive/Press Association Images; p.39 © Photodisc/Getty Images/World Commerce & Travel 5; p.41 © David Warren / Alamy; p.42 © Rex Features; p.47 KeystoneUSA-ZUMA/Rex Features; p.48 (left) © Rex Features, (right) © Jordi Matas / Demotix/Demotix/ Press Association Images; p.50 © Christopher Furlong/AP/Press Association Images; p.51 © NUS; p.52 © Jamie Wiseman / Npa Rota /Rex Features; p.53 (top) © PA/PA Archive/Press Association Images, (bottom left) © Rex Features, (bottom right) © Rex Features; p.55 © Tim Graham/Getty Images; p.56 © PA Wire/PA Archive/Press Association Images; p.60 (left) © Getty Images, (right) © The Conservative Party; p.61 (left) © Ray Tang/Rex Features, (right) © The Labour Party; p.62 (left) © David Hartley/Rex Features, (right) © Liberal Democrat Party; p.68 © STEVE LINDRIDGE / Alamy; p.69 © Andrew Milligan/PA Archive/Press Association Images; p.70 © Rex Features; p.72 © George Adam MSP; p.82 © AFP/Getty Images; p.88 (top) © Getty Images, (bottom) © Rex Features; p.93 © Stirling Council; p.94 © Alistair Dick / Fotolia.com; p.97 © Andrew Milligan/PA Wire/Press Association Images; p.100 © Diller Scofidio + Renfro / Keppie Design; p.102 (left) © The Scottish National Party, (right) © AFP/Getty Images; p.103 (top left) © The Scottish Labour Party, (top right) © The Scottish Conservative Party, (bottom left) © Danny Lawson/PA Archive/Press Association Images, (bottom right) © Getty Images; p.104 (top) © Scottish Liberal Democrat Party, (bottom) © Getty Images; p.108 © Rex Features; p.110 (left) © Mumsnet, (right) © Stefan Rousseau/PA Archive/Press Association Images; p.111 (left) © Ken Jack / Demotix/Demotix/Press Association Images, (right) © Campaign for Nuclear Disarmament; p.115 © Unison; p.117 (left) © London News Pictures/Rex Features, (right) © Crawford Brown/Rex Features; p.118 © Getty Images; p.121 © Andrew Milligan/PA Archive/Press Association Images; p.122 (top both) © NI Syndication, (bottom) © NI Syndication; p.124 © Ken McKay/ITV/Rex Features; p.127 (both) © Frank Cooney; p.128 © David Sheerin; p.130 © David Sheerin.

Acknowledgements Page 102 Copyright Guardian News & media Ltd 2012. Extracts from the National 4 Modern Studies Course Specification (p.132), National 4 Added Value Unit Specification (p.135), National 5 Modern Studies Course Specification (p.137) and National 5 Modern Studies Course Support Notes (p.142) are reproduced with the permission of the Scottish Qualifications Authority.

Every effort has been made to trace all copyright holders, but if any have been inadvertently overlooked the Publishers will be pleased to make the necessary arrangements at the first opportunity.

Although every effort has been made to ensure that website addresses are correct at time of going to press, Hodder Gibson cannot be held responsible for the content of any website mentioned in this book. It is sometimes possible to find a relocated web page by typing in the address of the home page for a website in the URL window of your browser.

Hachette UK's policy is to use papers that are natural, renewable and recyclable products and made from wood grown in sustainable forests. The logging and manufacturing processes are expected to conform to the environmental regulations of the country of origin.

Orders: please contact Bookpoint Ltd, 130 Park Drive, Abingdon, Oxon OX14 4SE. Telephone: (44) 01235 827720. Fax: (44) 01235 400454. Lines are open 9.00–5.00, Monday to Saturday, with a 24-hour message answering service. Visit our website at www.hoddereducation.co.uk. Hodder Gibson can be contacted direct on: Tel: 0141 848 1609; Fax: 0141 889 6315; email: hoddergibson@hodder.co.uk

© Frank Cooney, Gary Hughes and David Sheerin 2013

First published in 2013 by

Hodder Gibson, an imprint of Hodder Education,
An Hachette UK Company
2a Christie Street
Paisley PA1 1NB

Impression number   5 4 3

Year   2017 2016 2015 2014

Cover photo © Heartland-Fotolia

Illustrations by Emma Golley at Redmoor Design and Integra Software Services Pvt. Ltd

Typeset in 11 on 14pt ITC Stone Serif Medium by Integra Software Services Pvt. Ltd., Pondicherry, India.

Printed in Dubai

A catalogue record for this title is available from the British Library

ISBN: 978 1444 182 224

Contents

Chapter 1

Living in a democracy

What is a democracy?

What are the features of a democracy?

In a democracy such as the UK, citizens can participate freely through voting to elect their political representatives, usually from a list of candidates representing political parties such as Labour, Conservative, Liberal Democrat and, in Scotland, the Scottish National Party (SNP). We have also the right to free speech, to join pressure groups and trade unions and to criticise the government. We expect our newspapers and television (mass media) to provide us with information and informed opinion to enable us to make up our minds who we will vote for at an election. We may take these rights for granted, but in many countries people live in a dictatorship. In Burma a limited number of free elections were held in April 2012, the first since 1990.

> **What you will learn:**
>
> 1 The UK is a representative democracy.
> 2 The rights and responsibilities of living in a democracy.
> 3 The nature of the political system in the UK.

Figure 1.1 Aung San Suu Kyi celebrating in April 2012

Democracy returned to Burma when the party of Aung San Suu Kyi won 43 of the 45 by-election seats in April 2012. The last free elections had been held in 1990. Aung San won that election too but the army refused to accept the result and placed Aung San under house arrest. Only in November 2010 was she allowed to leave her home. She is loved by her people, and the army dictatorship only control the country through fear and punishment.

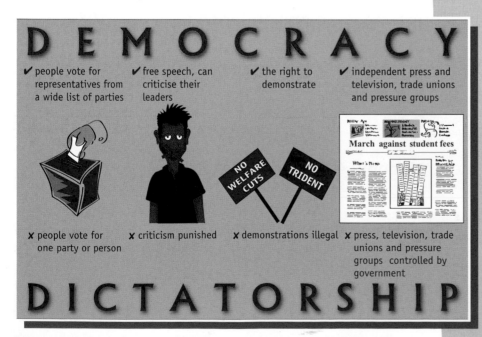

Figure 1.2 The differences between democracy and dictatorship

Rights	Responsibilities
To elect our representatives and vote on issues such as Scottish independence.	To accept the decision of the majority even if we disagree.
To vote in an election when aged 18 or over.	To be responsible citizens and use our vote in an attempt to influence our representatives.
To express our views in speech and in print, on social networking sites and by writing to newspapers.	To avoid telling lies or slandering individuals, since this is illegal.
To protest and try to change government legislation such as the recent increases in student fees in England and Wales.	To protest within the law and respect the rights of others.

Table 1.1 Our rights and responsibilities in a democracy

In South Africa the majority Black African population received the vote only in 1994 when Nelson Mandela became the first president of the newly democratic South Africa.

We have all these political rights but we have the responsibilities to use these rights wisely, as Table 1.1 indicates. A right is something a person is entitled to, and responsibilities are things that people should do or are expected to do.

Show your understanding

1 What are the most important features of a democracy?
2 Copy out the rights we have in the UK and, in your own words, explain the responsibilities that go with these rights.

ICT task

Working in pairs, find out more about Aung San Suu Kyi and explain why she won the Nobel Peace Prize. Create a 3–5 slide presentation to report back to your class.

The UK political system

The UK is a parliamentary democracy with a constitutional monarch. The Queen is head of state to the peoples of England, Scotland, Northern Ireland and Wales, and to the peoples of the 15 realms of the Commonwealth. In 2012 the Queen celebrated her diamond jubilee, commemorating 60 years on the British throne.

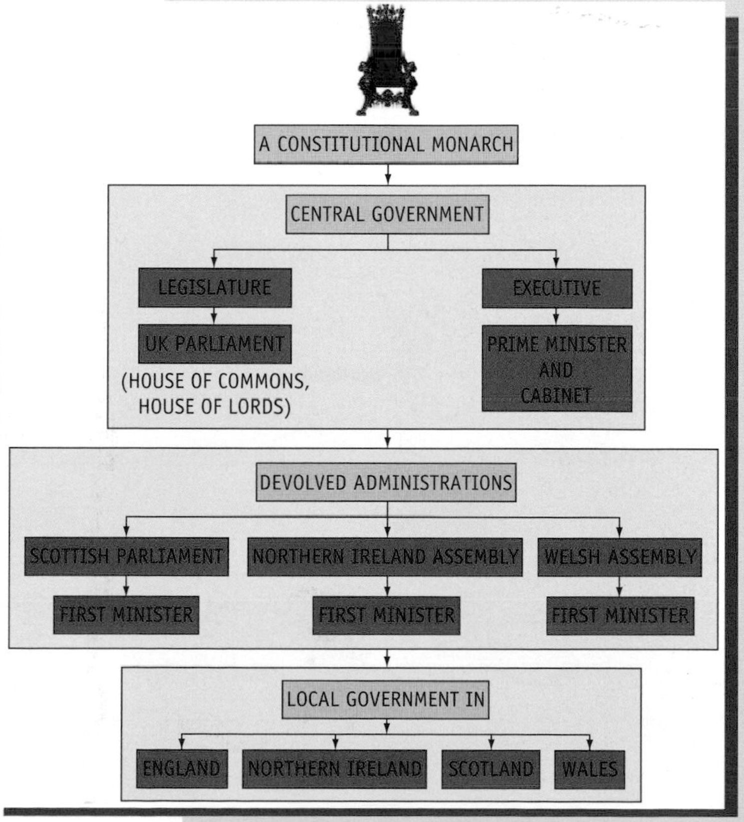

A CONSTITUTIONAL MONARCH

CENTRAL GOVERNMENT

LEGISLATURE

UK PARLIAMENT

(HOUSE OF COMMONS, HOUSE OF LORDS)

EXECUTIVE

PRIME MINISTER AND CABINET

DEVOLVED ADMINISTRATIONS

SCOTTISH PARLIAMENT   NORTHERN IRELAND ASSEMBLY   WELSH ASSEMBLY

FIRST MINISTER   FIRST MINISTER   FIRST MINISTER

LOCAL GOVERNMENT IN

ENGLAND   NORTHERN IRELAND   SCOTLAND   WALES

Figure 1.3 The structure of the UK political system

Figure 1.3 illustrates Scotland's place in the UK political system. The traditional **prerogative powers** of the monarch are held by the UK prime minister and cabinet. **Parliamentary sovereignty** ensures all powers are vested in Parliament and the powers granted to the devolved governments can in theory be returned to the UK Parliament.

The UK government is directly accountable to Parliament – the governing party (or parties) is only in power because it has a majority of seats in the House of Commons, and at any time the government can be dismissed by the Commons through a vote of 'no confidence'. This seldom happens and last occurred in 1979 when the Labour government of James Callaghan was dismissed by the House of Commons. It is now even more difficult for Parliament to dismiss the government as the Conservative–Liberal Democrat coalition government passed a law in September 2011 which requires at least 55% of MPs' votes to be 'no confidence' – not a simple majority – in order to force a government to resign. Members of the government are also Members of Parliament and this fusion of powers usually ensures the UK Executive (government) dominates the legislature (parliament).

In the London 2012 Olympics the UK was referred to by the British media as Team GB. (The foreign media often referred to the British team as England, as many assume that England and Britain mean the same.) The term Team GB is not quite accurate, as Great Britain is the geographical name for mainland Scotland, England and Wales, not including Ireland. United Kingdom is short for the United Kingdom of Great Britain and Northern Ireland. So, to be strictly accurate, we should refer to the British team as Team GB, Northern Ireland and Crown Dependencies.

Constitution: A parliamentary committee defined a constitution as 'the set of laws, rules and practices that creates the basic institutions of the state and its ... related parts, and stipulates the powers of those institutions and the relationship between the different institutions and between those institutions and the individual.' The UK does not have a single written constitution.

Royal prerogative: Powers of the monarch that are exercised in the Crown's name by the prime minister and government ministers.

Parliamentary sovereignty: The UK Parliament has absolute authority as it is the supreme law-making body in Great Britain. However, membership of the European Union and acceptance of the 1998 Human Rights Act set out in the European Convention on Human Rights (ECHR) can now place limits on Parliament's supremacy.

Figure 1.4 The United Kingdom

Figure 1.5 Democracy as we know it began in ancient Athens

How are decisions made in the UK?

In ancient Greece, the birthplace of democracy, the male citizens of Athens voted on all decisions of government (direct democracy). The word 'democracy' derives from two Greek words, *demos* (people) and *kratia* (rule). Obviously, direct democracy would not work in the modern world. The UK has a population of 60 million, and within that Scotland has 5.2 million. It would be impossible for every UK citizen, or every Scottish citizen, to meet and express their individual points of view. The nearest action to direct democracy is when the government asks the people to make a decision in what is called a **referendum** (see page 9).

Representative democracy

We participate by electing individuals to represent our views, and these representatives take decisions on our behalf. If we do not approve of their actions we simply vote for a different representative, who is called a candidate, at the next election. Our preferred candidate may not be elected but we must accept the majority decision.

As Figure 1.6 indicates, we choose a range of representatives. At the local level we elect over 1200 **local councillors** every four years to represent us and to administer the local council for the area we live in (see pages 89–101). Local councillors look after services such as education, housing, roads and refuse collection.

Figure 1.6 People who represent us

Since 1999 we now have a Scottish Parliament and we elect 129 **Members of the Scottish Parliament (MSPs)** and a Scottish government every four years to be responsible for the **devolved powers** given by the UK Parliament. Some of these devolved powers concern education, health care and law and order (see Table 1.2, page 8 and page 79). The UK government decides each year how much money it will give to the Scottish Parliament, and the Scottish government can decide how it wishes to spend the money (see Chapter 3).

At least once every five years we take part in a UK general election, which is held throughout the United Kingdom (England, Scotland, Wales and Northern Ireland) to elect 650 **Members of Parliament (MPs)** and a UK government. The House of Commons and the UK government make decisions on such issues as the economy, taxation, foreign affairs and defence. These are **reserved powers**.

Finally, Scottish voters, as part of the United Kingdom, choose every five years our six **Members of the European Parliament (MEPs)**. In the 2009 European elections the citizens of the 27 member states of the European Union elected 736 MEPs (see page 24).

Figure 1.7 The European Parliament in Strasbourg

Devolution and Scotland's future

This is an exciting time to be studying Scotland and its place in the UK political system. The SNP majority Scottish government intends to hold a referendum in 2014 to ask the Scottish people if they wish to have independence and leave the UK political system. The UK government would prefer to hold a referendum before 2014 and the Scottish Labour, Conservative and Liberal Democrat parties will all campaign against independence.

Elections were held in 1999 to set up a Scottish Parliament with devolved powers on matters such as education and health care. The UK Parliament has sole authority over 'reserved matters' such as social security and defence and could dissolve the Scottish Parliament. However, the SNP and others

claim that Westminster parliamentary sovereignty is an English doctrine and regard popular sovereignty as central to Scottish political traditions. In 2012 further powers were transferred from Westminster to Holyrood, such as the right to reduce alcohol limits for driving and to set national speed limits. Some commentators argue that what Scotland needs is not independence but greater powers for the Scottish Parliament – this is referred to as **devomax**. Chapter 3 on Democracy in Scotland examines the impact of devolution on Scottish politics and society.

Devolved matters	Reserved matters
Health	Defence
Education and training	Social security
Social work	Foreign affairs
Housing	Constitutional matters
Local government	Immigration
Tourism and economic development	Broadcasting
Law and home affairs	Trade and industry
Agriculture, forestry and fishing	Energy: nuclear, coal and gas
Planning	Employment legislation
Police and fire services	Equal opportunities
The environment	Fiscal and monetary system
Sports and the arts	Gambling and National Lottery
Scottish road network and harbours	Data protection

Table 1.2 Devolved and reserved powers

Referenda

A referendum (the plural is referenda) is a ballot in which voters, not their representatives in Parliament, pass judgement on a particular issue. It is a form of direct democracy because it involves citizens directly in decision making. A referendum can resolve important constitutional affairs or divisions within the government or among the public. In May 2011 the Conservative/Liberal Democrat Government held a referendum on electoral reform. The proposal to end the First Past The Post (FPTP) system of electing representatives and to replace it with the Alternative Vote (AV) system was defeated by a vote of 67.9% (no) to 32.1% (yes).

Critics of referenda argue that they undermine our UK system of representative democracy. We should allow our elected representatives to make the decisions on our behalf. They also point out that if there is a low turnout, the outcome may be decided by a small section of the community: for example, only 34.1% of the London electorate turned out to vote in the 1998 referendum on having a Mayor of London.

Issue	Turnout (%)	Yes (%)	No (%)
Scottish Devolution (1997)	60.4	74.3	25.7
Belfast Agreement (1998)	81.1	71.1	28.9
London Mayor (1998)	34.1	72.0	28.0
North East Regional Assembly (2004)	47.7	22.1	77.9
Alternative Vote	41.0	32.1	67.9

Table 1.3 Recent UK referenda results

Show your understanding

1 Explain why direct democracy is not possible in today's world.
2 What is a representative and why do we elect so many in Scotland today?
3 What is a referendum? Give three examples.
4 Explain the terms 'reserved powers' and 'devolved powers', and give two examples of each.

Branch out

5 An American visitor is confused about the nature of the UK political system. In pairs create a leaflet that explains the UK political system and explains why he should not call our country England.

Develop your skills

6 'The British people clearly support the use of referenda and this is reflected in a high turnout.' *(Rachael McLaren)* Using Table 1.3, explain why Rachael McLaren could be accused of exaggeration.

What you will learn:

1 The ways in which people can participate in Scottish and UK elections.
2 The range of elections that the public can vote in.
3 The main features of the different election systems used.
4 The strengths and weaknesses of the UK and Scottish electoral systems.

Electing representatives

How do we take part in elections?

As you are aware, we take part in elections to select our representatives at many different levels and with different electoral systems. In the past, Britain had only one electoral system, First Past The Post (FPTP), and this was used to elect MPs to the House of Commons, councillors to local councils across the UK and representatives to the European Parliament.

However, this is no longer the case. As Table 1.4 indicates, a variety of Proportional Representation (PR) systems now operate within the UK for various elections. In Scotland we elect local councillors using the Single Transferable Vote (STV), a form of PR; we elect our representative to the European Parliament using the Regional List, also a form of PR; we elect Members of the Scottish Parliament (MSPs) using the Additional Member System (AMS) – a mixture of FPTP and PR; and finally, we elect our Members of Parliament to the UK Parliament using FPTP.

So it is no surprise that there is great debate about what system is best for Britain. What should an election deliver? Should it be an FPTP system that usually helps to deliver a clear winner and strong

FACT FILE

Election day

In the 2010 general election an identical process took place in all of the 650 constituencies.

- To be eligible to vote your name must be on the Electoral Register – a form is sent out to all households every year asking who lives there.
- You will receive a polling card through the post which tells you where to vote and when.
- Voting hours are from 7a.m. to 10p.m.
- You can apply for a postal vote if you are not able to attend the polling station.
- At the polling station, usually a primary school, you will be given a ballot paper after your details have been checked.
- You will go into the polling booth and place a cross (X) beside the name of only one candidate, and then place your completed ballot paper into a sealed and locked box. For a local government or Scottish Parliament election, the voting procedure is slightly more complicated and this created problems in the 2007 elections (see page 18).
- Ballot boxes are collected and taken to a central point for the ballot papers to be counted.

System	Election of:	Constituency type
First Past The Post (FPTP)	House of Commons	Single
	Local government	
	Councils in England and Wales	
Additional Member System (AMS) (FPTP and AMS)	Scottish Parliament	Single and multi-member
	Welsh Assembly	
	London Assembly	
Regional List (PR)	European Parliament (not Northern Ireland)	Multi-member
Single Transferable Vote (STV) (PR)	Scottish local government councils	Multi-member
	Northern Ireland Assembly	
	Northern Ireland European Parliament	

Table 1.4 Electoral systems in the UK

government and maintains an effective link between MPs and geographical constituencies? Or should it be a PR system that helps to ensure greater proportionality and fairness between votes cast and seats achieved?

Yet something very strange happened in the 2010 general election and 2011 Scottish Parliament elections, which perhaps weakened the argument for FPTP and strengthened the argument for AMS. The 2010 general election failed to deliver its main strength – a clear overall majority for one party – and in the 2011 election the SNP achieved what was thought impossible – a clear overall majority for the winning party. The perceived weakness of AMS – that it delivers only coalition or minority government – no longer applied.

Figure 1.8 Voting on election day

www

www.aboutmyvote.co.uk/how_do_i_vote/polling_station_walkthrough.aspx

Ways in which local party workers participate in election campaigns

I deliver leaflets to people's doors with our party's promises and a picture of our candidate, and I hand them out in the main shopping areas.

I support the candidate doing walkabouts in the main shopping areas, shaking hands with the public and engaging in debate.

I put up bright posters with our party's name, logo and a picture of the candidate on lampposts and hand out stickers and rosettes.

I put a loudspeaker on my car to participate in a cavalcade around the local area urging the public to vote for our candidate.

On election day I take elderly supporters to vote and also take my turn to stand outside a polling station to display support for our party and candidate.

What is a candidate?

A candidate is an individual who wants to be elected to a local council or to the Scottish or UK or European Parliament. Most candidates belong to one of the main political parties – Labour, SNP, Conservative or Liberal Democrat – or minority parties such as the Green Party.

The local party will interview and select a candidate, who must be 18 or over. Taking part in an election campaign is expensive and those who stand as an Independent are seldom elected. Each candidate must pay a deposit of £500 and if they fail to receive 5% of the votes they lose the money.

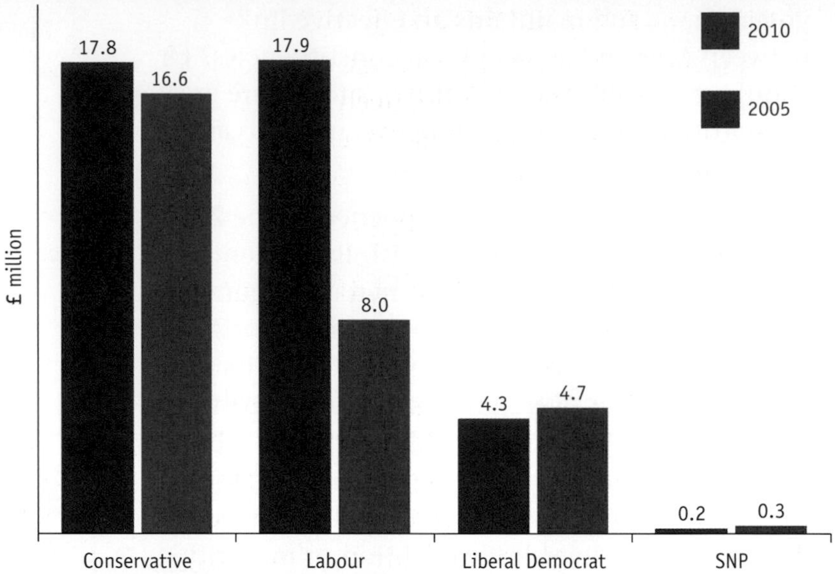

Figure 1.9 Campaign spending by selected parties in the 2005 and 2010 UK general elections

The Election Campaign

A general election has to be held every five years and elections for the Scottish Parliament every four years. Until recently the prime minister could hold an election at any time. (Gordon Brown became prime minister after Tony Blair's resignation in 2007 and perhaps later regretted not holding an election that year or the next; he lost the election in 2010.) However, under the coalition government's new agreement, Parliament will have a fixed term of five years and the next election will be in May 2015.

During elections, supporters of candidates, usually party members, do their best to persuade voters to elect their candidate. In national elections the main campaign is fought using old and new technology. Television and newspapers provide opportunities for the party leaders to explain their policies and to criticise the other leaders. Facebook and Twitter are used to enable candidates to engage with the public. Parties spend a large amount of money in advertising and travelling around constituencies, especially those in which they have a chance of winning (see Table 1.5).

Party	Spending (£)
Conservative and Unionist	273,462
Labour	816,889
Liberal Democrat	176,300
SNP	1,141,662

Table 1.5 Campaign spending by selected parties, 2011 Scottish Parliament elections

WWW
For further information go to www.electoralcommission.org.uk/party-finance/party-finance-analysis

Who is not allowed to vote ?

Those who are under 18. However, in some countries those aged 16 and over can vote (See the voting age debate on pages 13–14).

Members of the Royal Family

Individuals who have been declared bankrupt

Individuals with severe mental health problems

Prisoners. However, the European Court of Human Rights has requested that UK prisoners be allowed to vote.

Voting turnout and voting age

In the first part of this chapter we saw that many people around the world cannot freely choose their elected representatives. In China, for example, people have a vote but can only vote for the Chinese Communist party. When students occupied Tiananmen Square in 1989 and demanded the democratic right to have free and open elections, government tanks and troops massacred the protesters. Yet in the UK today there has been a serious decline, especially among young people, in voting at elections. In the 2005 general election only 59.4% of the electorate turned out to vote. The 2010 election did see an increased turnout, of 65%. However, it was still far below the post-war average of 78%.

Apathy and disillusionment

It is clear that many citizens are dissatisfied with the political parties, and the scandal about MPs' expenses in 2009 has further reduced public confidence and created greater disillusionment. Table 1.6 clearly shows that young people especially are less inclined to vote. Youth unemployment is at a record high and many feel betrayed by politicians. In their 2010 election promises (**manifesto**) the Liberal Democrats had promised to oppose an increase in university fees and they won the most votes in the 18–24 age group. Yet when the Liberal Democrats joined the coalition government in 2010 they supported an increase in student fees. Young people may be disillusioned by the action of the Liberal Democrats and may be less inclined to vote in future elections.

Should the voting age be reduced to 16?

The Electoral Reform Society and the think tank Demos favour the reduction of the voting age to 16. Demos claims that one million people aged 16–17

Age group	Turnout (%)
18–25	44
65+	76

Table 1.6 Voting turnout by age in the 2010 general election

are denied the vote because of outdated attitudes. This group of citizens can get married, raise a family, pay their taxes and fight and die for their country, yet cannot vote. Others argue that 16- and 17-year-olds lack maturity and life experience, and if they are given the vote this will only decrease still further the low percentage turnout of young people. The Liberal Democrats, the Greens and the SNP support lowering the voting age. The SNP in its 2012 *Your Scotland – Your Referendum* consultation document reiterate their wish to include in the referendum bill legislation to enable 16- and 17-year-olds to vote in the referendum on Scottish independence. This would increase the electorate by about 125,000. The Edinburgh Agreement of October 2012 (see page 83) between David Cameron and Alex Salmond includes the right of 16- and 17-year-olds to vote.

Figure 1.10 Old enough to fight but not to vote?

> Of the first 100 British soldiers to die in Iraq, at least six were too young to vote in a general election.

Richard Reeves, Demos

> All sections of Scottish society will come together to choose Scotland's future and independence in the referendum. It is only right that young folk who can legally marry and join the army should have their say.

Alex Salmond, First Minister

Views of students St Ninian's High School, Kirkintilloch

Figure 1.11 Andrew Finlayson, aged 15

I think that the voting age should be reduced from 18 to 16 years old. There are many things you can do at the age of 16 but voting isn't one of them. You can get married, join the army etc. What the government is literally saying is that you can go and die for your country but you are not allowed to vote! It doesn't make sense. If the age is lowered to 16, young people will be interested in voting.

I would like to vote in the Scottish independence referendum. I think I am mature and intelligent enough to make an informed decision. It's our country, our land and I should have a say.

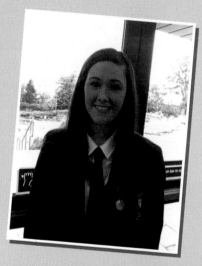

Figure 1.12 Lisa Flaherty, aged 16

Even though I believe 16-year-olds should have some control over their own future as they contribute to society, I do not agree that they should be able to vote. I believe there is apathy among young voters – already 18–24-year-olds have the lowest turnout. 16-year-olds are likely to follow suit and not vote, therefore it would be a waste of money. I think parents of 16-year-olds should vote on behalf of their children.

ICT task

Working in pairs, research the website www.votesat16.org, the site of the Votes at 16 campaign. Create a slide presentation, with between three and five slides, to present to your class.

Show your understanding

1   Describe the electoral systems used in the UK.
2   What was unusual about the 2010 general election and the 2011 Scottish Parliament election?
3   What is a candidate, and which parties and causes might candidates represent?
4   Describe the ways that party members and individuals can participate during an election campaign.
5   Explain why not everyone over the age of 18 is allowed to vote.
6   Outline the arguments for and against lowering the voting age to 16.

Branch out

7   In pairs, discuss the arguments for and against prisoners being allowed to vote. Create a poster either for or against prisoners having the right to vote.
8   Again working in pairs, create a poster for or against the voting age being lowered to 16.

Develop your skills

9   'Both the Labour and Conservative parties had roughly the same campaign budget for the 2005 and 2010 general elections.' *(Shabaz Mirza)* Using Figure 1.9 on page 12, explain why Shabaz Mirza could be accused of exaggeration.

Coalition: joining together of two or more political parties to form a government.

Opposition: the second-largest party in the House of Commons. The opposition has a key role in scrutinising the government.

Party manifesto: a public declaration of policy and aims, usually issued before an election by a political party.

UK electoral systems

As we have seen, the British electoral system for the House of Commons is known as First Past The Post, also called a 'simple majority' system. The UK is divided into 650 constituencies, also known as seats, and each one elects a Member of Parliament (MP). The candidate who wins the most votes becomes the MP, and Table 1.7 explains why it is called the 'winner takes all' system. In the 2010 general election Glenda Jackson (Labour) won the Hampstead and Kilburn seat with only 42 votes more than the Conservative candidate – 67.2% of the electorate did not vote for the winning candidate.

Usually the party which has the most MPs has an overall majority in the House of Commons (this requires a minimum of 326 seats) and will form the new government. However, in 2010 no party gained an overall majority (see Table 1.8) and so the largest party, the Conservatives, invited the Liberal Democrats to become part of the government. This is referred to as a **coalition government**. Labour, as the second largest party, became the official **opposition** party.

Party	Candidate	Share of votes (%)
Labour	Glenda Jackson	32.8
Conservative	Chris Philp	32.7
Liberal Democrat	Edward Fordham	31.2
Other		3.3

Table 1.7 Hampstead and Kilburn constituency, general election 2010

Party	Seats	Change from previous election	Votes (%)	Seats (%)
Conservative	307	+97	36.1	47.2
Labour	258	−91	29.0	38.7
Liberal Democrat	57	−5	23.0	8.9

Table 1.8 UK general election result 2010, main UK parties (Great Britain)

Party	Seats	Change from previous election	Votes (%)
England			
Conservative	298	+92	39.5
Labour	191	−87	28.1
Liberal Democrat	43	−4	24.2
Scotland			
Conservative	1	0	16.7
Labour	41	0	42.0
Liberal Democrat	11	0	18.9
Wales			
Conservative	8	+5	26.1
Labour	26	−4	36.3
Liberal Democrat	3	−1	20.1

Table 1.9 General election results 2010 by area, main UK parties (Great Britain)

FACT FILE

Summary of 2010 general election

- The Conservatives gained 87 seats from Labour and 12 from the Liberal Democrats.
- Labour's 29% share of the UK vote was only slightly better than the party's post-war low in 1983.
- The drift away from the 'old two-party system' continued; only two in three of all votes cast were for the two major parties.
- Five million fewer people voted for Labour, compared to the 1997 Labour landslide victory.
- The number of ethnic minority MPs increased from 14 to 27.
- The Conservatives failed once again to make progress in Scotland. The Conservatives remained the fourth placed party, with only one MP.
- The Green Party elected their first MP, Caroline Lucas. All three sitting Independent MPs were defeated.

First Past The Post (FPTP)

Maintains a two-party system

FPTP ensures that the seats achieved by Conservative and Labour are far greater than the proportion of votes they receive. In the 2010 general election the combined Conservative/Labour vote was 65.1%, yet they received 85.9% of the seats (see Table 1.8).

Comfortable government

FPTP usually exaggerates the performance of the most popular party and provides it with a comfortable majority in Parliament. The Conservatives under Margaret Thatcher had landslide victories in 1983 and 1987, as did Labour under Tony Blair in 1997 and 2001. However, this did not happen in the 2010 general election.

Unfair to smaller parties

FPTP discriminates against third parties and small parties whose support is spread across the UK but is not concentrated in particular regions. The Liberal Democrats have consistently suffered, as there are no rewards for coming second – even if this happened in, say, 300 constituencies. In the 2010 general election, the Liberal Democrats won 23% of votes but only received 57 seats. In contrast, Labour won 29% of votes and received 258 seats. The Green Party did manage to win their first-ever seat in the 2010 election.

Limited choice

Many constituencies are **safe seats** in which one party has a massive majority over its rivals and is unlikely to lose. All of Glasgow's constituencies are held by Labour, and the Conservatives do very badly. Why should a Conservative voter bother to vote when his/her vote will be of no consequence?

Figure 1.13 Caroline Lucas became the first member of the Green Party to be elected to the UK Parliament.

Alternative Vote (AV)

This was the proposed electoral system, to replace FPTP, of the Conservative–Liberal Democrat coalition. This seemed a strange choice for the Liberal Democrats, as AV is, in effect, only a modified form of FPTP.

AV is used to elect Australia's lower house, the House of Representatives, and in the UK it is used to elect the leaders of the Labour and Liberal Democrat parties.

In AV the winning candidate has to achieve an overall majority of the votes cast. Voters write 1 beside the name of their first choice, 2 next to their second choice and so on. Voters may decide to vote only for their first choice. If no candidate has secured an absolute majority of first preferences, the lowest-placed candidate drops out and the second preferences of his or her votes are transferred to the remaining candidates. If this does not produce a candidate with more than 50% of the votes, the procedure will be repeated until it does.

Arguments for First Past The Post

1 It usually provides strong single-party government and allows the prime minister and cabinet to pursue policies clearly stated in their election manifesto, without having to compromise with smaller parties in the kind of coalitions associated with Proportional Representation (PR).

2 The system prevents extremist parties from obtaining representation. The British National Party (BNP) achieved over half a million votes in the 2010 general election but gained no seats. Under a PR system the BNP won two seats in the 2009 European elections.

3 When an MP retires or dies, a **by-election** is held to elect a new MP. This enables the public to show their disapproval of a government or party in government which has become unpopular. (For by-elections, see page 19.)

4 It is easy to understand and implement. Electors only vote once and the results are announced very quickly. In contrast, there were 140,000 spoilt ballot papers in the 2007 Scottish Parliament elections that used AMS.

Arguments against First Past The Post

1 It does not always deliver a decisive victory for one party and create strong and stable government. The Conservatives failed to gain an overall majority in the 2010 general election. They formed a coalition with the Liberal Democrats but the partners disagree over major issues such as welfare reform and reform of the House of Lords.

2 It can lead to a situation where the winning MP in a constituency can receive less than 30% of the vote. In 1992 the Liberal Democrat candidate in Inverness East, Nairn and Lochaber won with 26% of the vote (see also Table 1.7 on page 15).

3 It is argued that FPTP leads to voter apathy as FPTP can create electoral deserts. The Conservatives won 17% of the Scottish votes in 2010 but only one seat.

4 The number of seats gained in the House of Commons does not accurately reflect the percentages of votes for each of the parties.

 Show your understanding

1 Why is the UK electoral system called First Past The Post?
2 Describe the main features of FPTP and give evidence to support the view that it is unfair to the Liberal Democrats.
3 Choose two arguments for FPTP and two against. Explain why you feel these are the best arguments to support each side.

Branch out

4 In pairs, create a summary sheet of the key results of the 2010 general election.
5 Referring to page 19, what is a by-election and what was significant about the 2012 Bradford West by-election?

Develop your skills

6 'The Conservatives increased their number of seats in England and Wales in the 2010 election and had the most seats across all of Great Britain.' *(Pauline Kelly)*
   Using Tables 1.8 and 1.9, explain the extent to which Pauline Kelly could be accused of being selective in her use of facts.

By-elections

If an MP dies, retires or resigns before the next general election a by-election is held. This means the constituency will choose a new MP. By-elections tend to receive national as well as local publicity and can be used by the public as an opportunity to give their verdict on the government and main political parties. In March 2012, George Galloway won a resounding victory in the by-election in Bradford West on a platform against UK involvement in Iraq and Afghanistan. The voters were clearly unimpressed by the coalition parties and the Labour opposition. Respect gained a majority of 10,140 over Labour and the Liberal Democrats faced the humiliation of losing their deposit.

Figure 1.14 George Galloway won the Bradford West by-election in March 2012.

Candidate	Party	Votes	%	+/−%
George Galloway	Respect	18,341	55.9	+52.8
Imran Hussain	Labour	8,201	25.0	−20.3
Jackie Whiteley	Conservative	2,746	8.4	−22.7
Jeanette Sunderland	Liberal Democrat	1,505	4.6	−7.1

Table 1.10 Results of Bradford West by-election, March 2012 (selected political parties)

The Scottish electoral system

The voting system used to elect MSPs and local councillors is different from that used to elect MPs. The voting system used for Scottish Parliament elections is called the Additional Member System (AMS) and for local councils it is called the Single Transferable Vote (STV). Both are forms of Proportional Representation (PR). In PR systems there is a greater link between votes received and seats won.

Additional Member System (AMS)

This mixed electoral system has been used to elect the Scottish Parliament and Welsh Assembly since 1999, as well as the London Assembly. In Scotland the voters cast two votes. The first vote is to elect the 73 winning candidates in the local constituency elections using FPTP.

The voter also has a second vote in a multi-member constituency, choosing between parties. Scotland is divided into eight regional lists, each electing seven regional list MSPs (see Figure 1.15 on page 20). The d'Hondt formula is used to ensure that the number of seats for parties in the Scottish Parliament is roughly proportional to the number of votes they won. A party that has a clear lead in the constituency election will do less well in the regional list elections. In 2007 Labour won 37 constituency seats but only 9 regional list seats, and in 2011 the SNP won 53 constituency seats but only 16 regional list seats.

Until the 2011 election no party had won a majority of seats. This had ensured the creation of a

Labour–Liberal Democrat coalition government in Scotland after the 1999 and 2003 elections and of a minority SNP government after the 2007 election.

www

www.electoral-reform.org.uk/additional-member-system/ provides further information on AMS.

The impact of the new voting system

A fairer result

There is no doubt that AMS increases proportionality by reducing the gaps between shares of votes and seats. In sharp contrast, in 2010 the First Past The Post system awarded Labour almost 70% of Scottish seats in the House of Commons, with only 42% of the Scottish vote.

Usually coalition government or minority party government

In 1999 and 2003 Labour formed a coalition government with the Liberal Democrats.

In the 2007 election the SNP overtook Labour as the strongest party in the Scottish Parliament, but only by a single seat. The SNP formed a minority government and had to depend on other parties supporting their policies for the respective bills to be passed in the Parliament.

Small parties encouraged and sometimes rewarded

In 2003 the Greens and the Scottish Socialist Party (SSP) won 13 out of 56 seats in the second ballot. The presence of Green and SSP MSPs in the Scottish Parliament would not have been achieved under First Past The Post. However, in the 2007 and 2011 elections only the Greens, with two MSPs, represented the smaller parties.

Greater voter choice

There has been a large increase in the number of parties and individual candidates competing for seats in the second ballot. More than 20 parties participated in the 2011 elections.

The 2011 Scottish Parliament election

The 2011 election was a triumph for the SNP, who achieved a landslide victory that gave them an overall majority in the Scottish Parliament and an

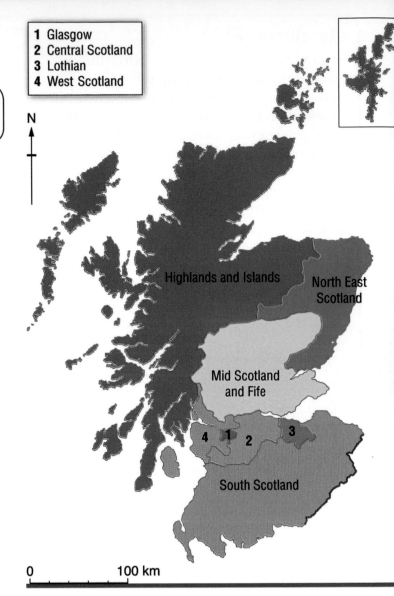

1 Glasgow
2 Central Scotland
3 Lothian
4 West Scotland

Figure 1.15 The eight regions in Scotland for Additional Member System elections

end to either coalition or minority government. Labour, who had maintained their dominance in the 2010 general election, suffered a collapse in their support and number of MSPs. Labour lost 9 seats while the SNP gained 22.

However, the biggest losers were the Liberal Democrats. Scottish voters were unhappy that the Liberal Democrats had joined up with the Conservatives to form a coalition government after the 2010 general election. The Liberal Democrats were punished and lost 11 of their 16 seats.

Arguments for Proportional Representation

1 PR is 'fair' because it produces a close correlation between shares of votes and shares of seats. In the Scottish Parliament 2011 elections, the Conservatives won about 13% of the votes and about 12% of the seats.

2 PR gives minor parties more parliamentary representation. In the 2003 elections for the Scottish Parliament, the Additional Member System (AMS) enabled the Scottish Socialist Party, the Green Party, the Scottish Senior Citizens Unity Party and the Independents to be represented.

3 Most European countries, such as Germany, use a form of PR.

4 Coalitions encourage consensus which is the result of compromise. In other words, more voters get some of what they want and less of what they do not want. The Liberal Democrats and Labour formed a coalition government in Scotland in the period 1999–2007, providing stable and effective government.

5 It is argued that PR will reduce the number of 'wasted votes' and so encourage greater turnout.

Arguments against Proportional Representation

1 PR can create a government in which a minority party can implement its policies. The Liberal Democrats finished fourth in the 2003 Scottish election, yet formed a government with Labour.

2 It can lead to unstable and weak government. The minority SNP government of 2007–2011 found it difficult to implement its policies. It failed, for example, to implement its policy of minimum pricing of alcohol in November 2010.

3 It does not always create a more representative Scottish Parliament. In the 2007 Scottish elections the number of MSPs outside the four major parties decreased from 17 to 3, with no change in the 2011 elections.

4 It is argued that AMS creates conflict between the constituency MSP and the seven list MSPs. There is clear rivalry between the two classes of MSPs.

5 It can lead to extremist parties gaining representation. In the 2009 European elections the British National Party (BNP) won two seats.

Party	SNP	+/−	Lab	+/−	Cons	+/−	Lib Dem	+/−	Other	+/−
Total	69	+22	37	−9	15	−2	5	−11	3	−

Table 1.11 Scottish Parliament election results, May 2011

Party	Seats	+/−	Votes	%	+/−%
SNP	53	+32	902,915	45.4	+12.5
Labour	15	−20	630,461	31.7	−0.5
Conservative	3	−3	276,652	13.9	−2.7
Liberal Democrat	2	−9	157,714	7.9	−8.2
Other	0	0	21,480	1.1	−1.1

Table 1.12 Scottish Parliament election May 2011, constituency results

Party	Seats	+/−	Votes	%	+/−%
SNP	16	−9	876,421	44.0	+13
Labour	22	−13	523,559	26.3	−2.9
Conservative	12	−2	245,967	12.4	−1.6
Liberal Democrat	3	−3	103,472	5.2	−6.1
Other	3	−1	241,632	12.1	−2.5

Table 1.13 Scottish Parliament election May 2011, regional list results

Show your understanding

1 Describe the main features of AMS.
2 Choose three arguments for AMS and three against. Explain why you feel these are the best arguments to support each side.

Branch out

3 In pairs, create a summary sheet of the key results of the 2011 Scottish elections.

Develop your skills

4 'The 2011 Scottish election was a triumph for the SNP and a total disaster for all other parties.' *(Catherine Healy)* To what extent does the evidence in Tables 1.11–1.13 support the view of Catherine Healy?

Figure 1.16 The BNP won their first-ever national representation in the European elections of 2009.

Single Transferable Vote (STV)

This PR system was used in the Scottish local government elections for the first time in May 2007. It is also used in Northern Ireland for elections to both the Northern Ireland Assembly and the European Parliament.

The main features of STV are:

- Representatives are chosen from multi-member constituencies.
- In a five-member local government constituency (ward), voters rank their preferences among the total number of candidates standing, using the numbers 1 to 5.
- Often the number of candidates will be in double figures.
- Electors can vote for as many or as few candidates as they like.
- A complicated quota system is used to calculate the minimum number of votes required to win one of the seats to be filled.

The local government elections 2007 and 2012

The introduction of the STV system in 2007 to replace FPTP has led to a fairer distribution of seats among the parties but it has also led to far fewer councils being controlled by one party. This results in a significant number of councils having coalition administrations. Labour dominance of local government has ended: in 2003, Labour had 509 councillors and overall control of 13 councils; SNP had 181 councillors and overall control of one council. In contrast, in the 2007 elections using STV, SNP gained the most councillors, having 363 but control of no councils, and Labour dropped to 348 councillors and control of two councils.

It was decided that elections for the Scottish Parliament and local councils would not take place at the same time, because of the number of spoilt ballots in the 2007 elections. For this reason, council elections were delayed until 2012. Both the SNP and Labour claimed that they were the winners in the 2012 council elections. The SNP could argue that they had the most seats and the largest increase in councillors. Labour could argue that they controlled the most councils, including Glasgow, which the SNP had hoped to win. What was clear was that the Liberal Democrats did badly – they lost 95 seats and suffered the humiliation of an Independent candidate dressed as a penguin receiving more votes than the Liberal Democrat candidate in Edinburgh's Pentland Hills ward – they came fourth behind 'the penguin' Professor Pongoo, a climate activist.

Party	Number of councillors	Net gain/loss compared with 2003 elections
Scottish National Party	363	+182
Scottish Labour	348	−161
Scottish Liberal Democrats	166	−9
Scottish Conservative	143	+20
Scottish Green	8	+8

Table 1.14 2007 local council election results

Party	Number of councillors	Net gain/loss compared with 2007 elections
Scottish National Party	425	+62
Scottish Labour	394	+46
Scottish Liberal Democrats	71	−95
Scottish Conservative	115	−28
Scottish Green	14	+6

Table 1.15 2012 local council election results

Party	2003 (FPTP)	2007 (STV)	2012 (STV)
Labour	13	2	4
SNP	1	0	2
Independents	6	3	4
Total councils	20	5	10

Table 1.16 Councils controlled by Labour, SNP, Independents

National/regional party list

This proportional representation system was introduced for elections to the European Parliament in England, Scotland and Wales in 1999 (but not in Northern Ireland). In this system the electorate do not vote for individual party candidates but for a party. Political parties draw up a list of candidates in the order in which they will be elected. Representatives are elected from 11 large multi-member regions, each electing between three and ten MEPs. In the 2009 European election Scotland elected six MEPs.

Some people may consider that a negative outcome of the PR nature of this election was the success of the British National Party in gaining two seats with only 6.2% of the votes.

Party	Votes		MEPs	
	Total	%	Total	+/−
Conservative	4,198,394	27.7 (+1.0)	25	+1
UK Independence Party	2,498,226	16.5 (+0.3)	13	+1
Labour	2,381,760	15.7 (−6.9)	13	−5
Liberal Democrats	2,080,613	13.7 (−1.2)	11	+1
Green Party	1,303,745	8.6 (+2.4)	2	0
British National Party	943,598	6.2 (+1.3)	2	+2
Scottish National Party	321,007	2.1 (+0.7)	2	0
Others	–	0.8	3	0

Note: Seats: 72; Turnout: 15,625,823; Electorate: 45,315,669.

Table 1.17 European Election 2009: UK results

Party	Votes total	Percentage	MEPs total
Scottish National Party	321,007	29.1	2
Labour	229,853	20.8	2
Conservative	185,794	16.8	1
Liberal Democrats	127,038	11.5	1
Green Party	80,442	7.3	0
UK Independence Party	57,788	5.2	0

Table 1.18 European Election 2009: Scotland

Show your understanding

1 Describe the main features of STV.
2 Outline the impact of the introduction of STV on the Scottish local council elections of 2007.
3 Explain how the national/regional list system operates. What weakness of PR did the 2009 European elections display?

Develop your skills

4 'The 2012 Scottish local government election was a triumph for the Labour Party, a disappointment for the SNP and Liberal Democrats, and a total disaster for all other parties.' *(Margaret Neil)*
Using Tables 1.14–1.16, explain why Margaret Neil could be accused of exaggeration.
5 Refer to Table 1.17 and Table 1.18. Why might Labour be disappointed with both its UK and Scottish performance?

Chapter 2

Democracy in the UK

The work of an MP

What is a Member of Parliament?

Members of Parliament (MPs) are representatives of everyone who lives in the UK. The UK is divided into geographical areas called constituencies and every constituency has its own MP. All MPs must serve their constituents (people who live in the constituency) well, whether a particular constituent actually voted for them or not. MPs must also serve those who cannot yet vote, such as schoolchildren. The average population of each constituency is around 69,000.

Once elected, an MP must serve the constituents until the next election. These elections are UK-wide and are known as general elections. General elections usually take place every five years. During this time an MP will divide their time between working in the constituency and working in London in Parliament. In 2012, MPs were paid £65,738 per year, plus allowances for travel, secretarial expenses and accommodation in London.

What you will learn:

1 The role of MPs in Parliament.
2 The role of MPs in their constituencies.
3 What challenges exist for MPs.
4 How women and ethnic minorities are represented in the UK Parliament.

Joanna Brown MP

At the general election Joanna Brown was elected to serve the Dalgeddie constituency as its Member of Parliament. Until the next general election in five years' time, her full-time job will be to represent her constituents in a number of ways. She needs to be willing to help individual constituents and local groups who have problems or concerns within the constituency. The constituents may also have concerns about wider national and international issues, such as the UK's involvement in wars or issues about taxation. She needs to listen to and understand these concerns, too, and to represent them in parliament.

Joanna Brown must ensure that she commits enough time to helping her constituents – she faces the prospect of losing at the next election if the constituents decide that she has not been successful in her role.

What does an MP do?

Put simply, an MP's job is to represent their constituents, whether a particular constituent voted for them or not. We live in a **representative democracy**, which means that MPs act as representatives of the general public. They act as the 'voice' of the people and they make decisions on our behalf. Every week each MP holds surgeries in their constituency, which are opportunities for constituents to meet them face to face and talk about problems they would like the MP to help with.

As every MP is elected, they must hold the government to account on our behalf and they also have the right to make decisions on our behalf. MPs carry out these duties by debating and voting on proposed laws, by asking questions of government ministers in Parliament and in public, and also by sitting on committees which will report on certain issues.

ICT task

1 Go to the website www.theyworkforyou.com.

2 Enter your home postcode in the 'Your representative' box. (If you do not know your own you can use your school's.)

3 Once your MP has been found, click on the link to their profile.

4 From the information on their profile page, complete the following tasks:

   a Voting record. List one occasion when your MP voted each of the following ways: strongly for, moderately for, for, against, moderately against, strongly against.

   b Topics of interest. Which government departments has your MP asked most questions about?

   c Numerology. How many times has your MP spoken in **debates** in the last year and how many **written questions** has your MP received answers to?

   d Expenses. List the figures for your MP's total expenses for the four most recent years shown.

Branch out

5 Write a paragraph explaining why you think all details of an MP's work should be published.

DIARY: JOANNA BROWN MP

Work in Parliament

Monday	Morning	Travel to London by train.
	Afternoon	Meet a representative from Amnesty International about support for a campaign to stop the conflict in the Middle East.
	Evening	Attend an adjournment debate in the House of Commons on changes to benefits.
Tuesday	Morning	Attend a debate about government plans for a new airport near my constituency.
	Afternoon	Sit on the cross-party Defence Committee on proposals to reduce nuclear weapons stocks.
	Evening	Attend a party meeting about strategy for the vote on Thursday.
Wednesday	Morning	Meet a group of schoolchildren from my constituency who are on a school trip for a tour of parliament.
	Afternoon	Attend Prime Minister's Question Time where I have been selected to present a question directly to the prime minister.
	Evening	Attend a debate on proposals to introduce a tax on unhealthy foods.
Thursday	Morning	Vote in the House of Commons on the government's bill to change pensions for the elderly.
	Afternoon	Travel to constituency by train.

Work in the constituency

Thursday	Afternoon	Arrive in constituency. Visit a local business that has created new jobs in the area.
	Evening	Attend a village meeting about the proposed location of the new airport.
Friday	Morning	Visit a local primary school to present awards. Meet a local constituent at her home to discuss the letter she wrote to me about noise in the area.
	Afternoon	Attend a meeting with local councillors regarding the decision to change rubbish collection to a fortnightly service.
	Evening	Turn on the new festival lights in Dalgeddie town centre.
Saturday	Morning	Attend surgery to meet constituents and hear their problems.
	Afternoon	Read all letters and emails passed to me by assistants at my constituency office.
	Evening	Family time!
Sunday	Morning	Visit the new football stadium of Rovers FC.
	Afternoon	Spend some time with family and friends.
	Evening	

As you can see, an average week for an MP is very busy and their time is divided between Parliament in London and activities within their constituencies.

Interview with Gregg McClymont MP

Gregg McClymont was elected as the Member of Parliament for Cumbernauld, Kilsyth and Kirkintilloch East following the 2010 general election. He was born and brought up in Cumbernauld and educated at Cumbernauld High School. Before entering politics he trained as a historian in Glasgow, Philadelphia and Oxford. He has a PhD from Oxford University, where he taught history until becoming an MP. He has been a member of the Labour Party all his adult life. In early 2011 he became an assistant whip (see page 38) before moving on to become the shadow pensions minister.

Why did you want to become an MP?

I grew up in the 1980s and developed a strong aversion to the government of the day. I thought things didn't have to be like this and that society could be much fairer. Being an MP gives me a platform to stand up for what I believe in and to try to improve the lives of my local constituents who come to me for help and advice.

What do you feel is the most effective task you can complete in Parliament?

As an elected opposition MP I am able to hold the government to account through debates, statements, and questions (written and oral). Making the government explain its policies to Parliament and representing my constituents' interests is my dual role.

How do you effectively manage your time in the constituency?

As an MP it's important to organise your time efficiently – especially since I usually only get back home from Parliament on a Thursday night. The staff in my constituency office do a fantastic job of organising my diary. They arrange

Figure 2.1 Gregg McClymont MP

appointments for me to meet constituents, and for those constituents that I cannot meet, they help deal with their issues, often calling and writing to government departments on my behalf to try to resolve constituents' problems. They also co-ordinate my work with local and national media. I would say that the demands on MPs are such that the constituency office is the key to effectively managing our time (see pages 36–38).

How do you balance the demands of your constituency and party?

That's a good question. I was elected as an MP because I was the Labour candidate, not because I'm Gregg McClymont! I am therefore always conscious of my party affiliation and the fact that nearly 25,000 people voted for me expecting me to take the Labour whip.

Diary: Gregg McClymont MP

Monday	7.30a.m.	Listen to BBC Radio 4's Today Programme or Radio Scotland and read the day's newspapers.
	9a.m.	Go to constituency office to check on emails and begin preparations for the day ahead.
	10.30a.m.	Fly to London from Glasgow Airport (spent Fri–Sun in my constituency).
	12.30p.m.	Go straight to Parliament from my flight and check on the status of my questions.
	1p.m.	Meet a High School group from my constituency who requested a tour of Parliament.
	1.30p.m.	Add my signature to a colleague's ten minute rule.
	1.45p.m.	Speak to the media – give a telephone interview to the **Cumbernauld News** over restoration of the historic landmark Cumbernauld House.
	2p.m.	Work and Pensions Question Time – ask the Secretary of State a question about public sector pensions.
	4p.m.	Meeting with pressure group and charity Age UK to discuss pensioner issues.
	6p.m.	Meeting with Parliamentary Labour Party; issued with the weekly whip.
	7p.m.	Due to make an application to the Backbench Committee but this is postponed due to a three-line whip on the government's plans to pass through Welfare Reform Bill at a division. No absences tolerated.
	8.30p.m.	Attend an adjournment debate in which I make a speech in Parliament.
	10p.m.	Finish my work for the day and head back to my London flat to prepare for tomorrow in Parliament.

1   How do MPs get elected and for how many years do they serve until the next election?
2   In your own words, describe the role of an MP.
3   Who do MPs work for?
4   What does the term 'representative democracy' mean?
5   Study the diary of Gregg McClymont MP shown on page 30.
    (a) In pairs, decide what you both consider to be the three most important tasks that need to be carried out and give reasons why, and each make a list of them.
    (b) In pairs, decide what is the most important **local** and the most important **national** issue and give reasons for your choice, and each note this down.

What types of tasks do MPs complete in Parliament?

MPs have a large number of commitments when they are in Parliament. There are some tasks that are almost compulsory to carry out, but many are at the MP's own discretion. This allows MPs to concentrate on the specific issues affecting their constituents and also issues which the MPs themselves have an interest in.

House of Commons business

The House of Commons is essentially a debating chamber, so much of the visible work that MPs carry out takes place at various debates. Debating allows MPs to carry out their role to **scrutinise** (look at in detail) the government and it also presents an opportunity for MPs to raise issues important to their local constituents.

Voting in the House

Perhaps the most important role of an MP is attending a vote in the House of Commons chamber. This is when, following the creation of a bill, MPs decide on whether it becomes a new law by individually voting 'aye' or 'no'. They make this decision officially on behalf of their constituency; however, MPs are influenced by many different people and groups so this decision is rarely straightforward. MPs will usually vote the way their political party wishes.

Adjournment debates

On a daily basis there are debates within the chamber. These present the opportunity for MPs to act as the 'voice' of the people. Debates are controlled by the Speaker. The Speaker is an MP who is chosen by fellow MPs to be the controller of the chamber. MPs are never guaranteed to be heard in an adjournment debate and must try to gain the attention of the Speaker by standing up when an opportunity presents itself, or waving papers. Quite often adjournment debates take place late at night, as on Mondays and Tuesdays Parliament does not finish working until 10p.m. These are known as End of Day adjournment debates.

Figure 2.2 MPs debating in the House of Commons

Question Time

Question Time is perhaps the most well-known business that MPs take part in: MPs get the opportunity to question a government minister about their department. Government ministers are MPs who are chosen by the prime minister to manage a government department, and key departments such as Health, Defence and the Environment have their own government ministers. According to a rota, each minister has to answer questions put forward by MPs for between 30 and 60 minutes. This allows MPs to scrutinise decisions that government ministers have made. There are strict rules over the submission of questions and most are 'seen' beforehand to allow the minister to prepare an answer. Questions are chosen by the Speaker of the House of Commons and as there is limited time for these debates, the vast majority of questions are not asked during the debate and instead get a written answer.

The prime minister has his or her own Question Time, which takes place every Wednesday. During this time the prime minister is questioned by MPs about the government's performance and may also be asked about how the government will respond to current events in the world such as conflicts, famine and poverty. How a government responds to different events can affect its popularity. This debate is also known as PMQs (Prime Minister's Questions), and often gets the most public attention of all the House of Commons business. Prime Minister David Cameron commented that PMQs is the 'most unpleasant looking thing that I have to do every week' and 'it is confrontational, adversarial and quite difficult to be anything else unless you want to get completely squashed by the other side'. Former Prime Minister Gordon Brown was seen as being unconvincing during PMQs, which seriously affected his leadership.

Written answers

Perhaps the most used but under-reported way in which MPs can represent their constituents is Written Answers. This is the process which allows an MP to write a question to a government department about an issue which is under its control. For example, an MP may write to the Environment Secretary regarding the government's thoughts about the environmental impact of building a new airport. The MP can then expect a written answer to the question within seven days. This is usually the method that MPs use to scrutinise the government and/or represent their constituents.

Figure 2.3 Prime Minister's Question Time

Committees

Most MPs will be a member of a committee in the House of Commons. This gives them an opportunity to research and have influence on a specific area or issue on which the government will make a decision. Most committees reflect the balance of power within the House of Commons; therefore, if a government has a large majority, it will have the majority of MPs on the committee. This may limit the committee's effectiveness in challenging the decision-making process. There are many different committees which look at different issues.

Select committees
Every government department has a select committee which scrutinises the work it carries out. The committees gather written evidence, interview experts and cross-examine witnesses. They then present their findings to the House of Commons. Their powers include compelling witnesses, including fellow MPs, to attend or produce records to help in their investigation. MPs are chosen by their fellow party members to be part of a select committee. This is a key way in which MPs can scrutinise the government.

Public bills committees
These committees act in a similar way to select committees in that they can call on witnesses and gather written evidence. The committee's main role is to develop and scrutinise planned government

Case study: Select committee on phone hacking

In 2011, the Culture, Media and Sport Select Committee held an inquiry into allegations made against the *News of the World* newspaper that it had, over a number of years, been hacking into the voicemails of politicians, celebrities and sports stars. Famous people such as singer Charlotte Church, actress Sienna Miller and publicist Max Clifford are thought to have had their phones hacked during this period. The committee, chaired by Conservative MP John Whittingdale, included nine other MPs.

The committee called upon *News of the World* owner Rupert Murdoch, his son James Murdoch and chief executive of the newspaper Rebekah Brooks. It was during one of these meetings that a protester called Jonnie Marbles attacked Rupert Murdoch with a foam pie, which triggered a huge security alert. The protestor shouted that Rupert Murdoch was a 'naughty billionaire', indicating that he disapproved of his company's alleged phone-hacking practices.

After hearing the three witnesses, including particularly strong questioning from Labour MP Tom Watson, it was revealed that the voicemail of schoolgirl Milly Dowler, who was murdered

Figure 2.4 Rupert Murdoch was attacked by a protestor while giving evidence at a Select Committee inquiry

in 2002, was hacked and her messages listened to while she was missing, which gave false hope to her parents and to the police that she was still alive. As a result of the investigation, the *News of the World* was closed down and Rebekah Brooks lost her job. The committee recommended to the House of Commons that a judicial inquiry should take place into ethics within the media. This was known as the Leveson Inquiry, which has made wide-ranging recommendations, including the creation of an independent body to monitor press standards which should be backed by legislation.

bills to assess their possible effects if they are passed into law. They then report their findings to the House of Commons before MPs decide on whether to vote 'aye' or 'no' to make the bill into law.

Backbench business committee
Introduced after the 2010 general election, this committee has the power to reserve space for debate in the House of Commons or Westminster Hall. It is also responsible for the government's e-petitions website: in an e-petition, any member of the public can highlight an issue and if the petition gains more than 100,000 signatures the committee will arrange for it to be debated by MPs. This was the case in October 2011, when 139,000 people had

signed an e-petition asking for MPs to debate the issues surrounding the Hillsborough disaster in 1989 in which 96 Liverpool Football Club supporters were killed due to poor crowd control.

ICT task

Go to http://epetitions.direct.gov.uk/

Look up some of the current open petitions. Remember that if a petition gains more than 100,000 signatures, the government has to respond.

Early Day Motions

Early Day Motions (EDMs) are formal proposals submitted for debate in the House of Commons. EDMs are used for reasons such as highlighting the views of individual MPs, drawing attention to specific events or campaigns, and showing if there is parliamentary support for a particular cause or point of view. Although there is very little prospect of an EDM actually being debated, many attract a great deal of public interest and frequently receive media coverage. Each EDM has a short title, for example 'School Food Standards', and a sentence no longer than 250 words detailing the motion.

Number of EDMs introduced	Number of EDMs with 100 signatures or more
3,024	96

Table 2.1 Early Day Motions 2010–12

Early Day Motions

EDM title: Trident Replacement

EDM date: 21 May 2012

EDM text: That this House notes the findings of the National Security Strategy that a nuclear weapon threat from another state is of low likelihood; further notes a procurement cost of £25 billion and an estimated lifetime cost of over £100 billion for the replacement of the Trident nuclear weapon system; believes that there are greater spending priorities both at the Ministry of Defence and across other departments; and urges the Government to cancel plans to replace Trident.

MP: Jeremy Corbyn MP for Islington North, Labour

Signatures: 89 MPs

Figure 2.5 A Royal Navy submarine armed with Trident nuclear missiles

EDM title: School Food Standards

EDM date: 14 May 2012

EDM text: That this House recognises the impact of unhealthy eating and obesity on children's health and well-being; expresses its concern that academies and free schools opened since September 2010 are not required to adhere to the mandatory standards for school food; welcomes the joint Jamie Oliver Children's Food Campaign, Food for Life Partnership, Local Authority Caterers Association and School Food Matters Save Our School Food Standards campaign; and calls on the Secretary of State to bring forward regulations to amend the Education (Nutritional Standards and Requirements for School Food) (England) Regulations 2007 to require academies and free schools to adhere to the standards for school food so that the one million children now attending these schools can benefit from this commitment to their health and well-being.

MP: Zac Goldsmith MP for Richmond Park, Conservative

Signatures: 107 MPs

Private members' bills

MPs who are not part of the cabinet have an opportunity to try to initiate their own bills. These are called private members' bills (PMBs). These bills rarely reach the later stages of the law-making process; however, they do form an important role undertaken by MPs. Perhaps the most famous private member's bill to become law is the Murder Act 1965, which abolished the death penalty in the UK.

Private members' bills can be introduced in three ways. At the beginning of the parliamentary year 20 applications for PMBs are selected at random to be debated for a whole day by the House of Commons. If an MP's bill is not selected, he or she will also have the opportunity to introduce it as a Ten Minute Rule bill, which allows an MP to speak for no longer than ten minutes about the issue surrounding their bill in order to gauge if their plans would gain enough interest. Lastly, a private member's bill can be introduced by a presentation to the House of Commons. Any MP can do this as long as notice is given; however, these presentations are usually poorly attended as they take place on Fridays, when most MPs are back in their constituencies.

 Show your understanding

1 For the following list of House of Commons business explain for each:
   (a) how MPs could represent their constituents **and**
   (b) why there are limits to their effectiveness in scrutinising the government.
     i Voting on a bill
     ii Adjournment debates
     iii Question Time
     iv Committees
     v Private members' bills
2 Describe the functions of the different committees available for MPs in the House of Commons.
3 Study the Case Study: Select committee on phone hacking. Explain how the committee used its powers and what effect they had on the media.
4 Explain in what ways MPs use the Ten Minute Rule.

Develop your skills

5 'In recent years the majority of EDMs have had strong support from fellow MPs and PMBs have become less successful.' (*Gerry Boyle*)

   Using Tables 2.1 and 2.2, explain to what extent Gerry Boyle could be accused of being selective in his use of the facts.

	Session	Number introduced	Number successful
Private members' bills	2011–12	52	3
	2010–11	78	4
	2009–10	67	7
Government bills	2010–12	39	39

Table 2.2 Private members' bills and government bills

What types of tasks do MPs do in their constituencies?

MPs have a large number of tasks to complete when they are present in their constituencies. For MPs, it is very important that they carry out as many tasks in their constituencies as they can because ultimately, at a general election, it is the people in their constituencies who have the power to re-elect them and to keep them in a job.

Attending meetings

MPs often meet with a wide variety of people in their local constituencies. Councillors, local organisations and local pressure groups all want to meet with MPs, in the hope that any issues they have can be raised at high levels of government. Equally, MPs want to meet these groups in order to stay up-to-date with issues affecting people in their constituencies. They also want to meet councillors in order to raise issues identified through communicating with constituents in letters, emails, social networking or meetings. They meet these people to talk about many different issues, such as the local environment and planned changes to local areas. A pressure group may want to try to persuade an MP to raise an issue or even want to get an MP's public support for their campaign.

Visits and social events

An MP is regarded as a high-profile guest by many organisations, and so MPs may spend a large proportion of their time attending various events – for example, the opening of a new business or an awards ceremony. Such events will often be reported in the local media and MPs often include details of these events in communications with their constituents. This provides an opportunity for MPs to raise their own profile in their constituencies and to represent all of their electorate.

Local party meetings

MPs meet occasionally with local party members to discuss issues which concern the party as a whole. The MP will then take this information back to the party's leadership. For most MPs, it is the local party members who will select them as a candidate at the

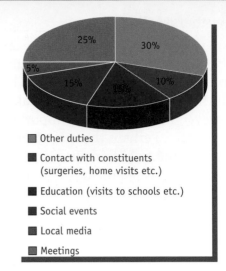

Other duties

■ Contact with constituents (surgeries, home visits etc.)

■ Education (visits to schools etc.)

■ Social events

■ Local media

■ Meetings

Figure 2.6 MPs' tasks in their constituencies

Figure 2.7 MPs spend half of their week in their constituencies.

next general election, and so MPs must maintain the support of this group of people.

Local media

In order to keep a good profile in their constituencies MPs often appear in local newspapers or on local TV and radio. This is an effective way of keeping potential voters aware of work done by MPs. Quite often MPs will raise awareness of local issues or highlight local charities using the media and communicate their thoughts about these issues. If an MP does not use the media effectively it could potentially damage their chance of re-election.

1   Why is it very important for MPs to carry out as many tasks as they can in their constituencies?
2   Explain the importance of each of the following activities done by MPs:
    (a) attending meetings
    (b) visits and social events
    (c) going to local party meetings
    (d) appearing in local media.

    For each activity give two examples to support your answer.

What opportunities exist for constituents to contact MPs directly?

All MPs receive a large volume of communications from their constituents. These can take the form of letters sent to Westminster or their constituency office; MPs constantly receive emails to their office email address; and most MPs now are in almost daily contact with constituents via social networking sites such as Twitter, Facebook and LinkedIn.

MPs have a small team of staff based at their constituency office who prioritise letters and emails. Increasingly, MPs are communicating directly with constituents via social networking. This allows MPs to keep up to date with events taking place in the constituency and to answer any queries while on the move. A good MP aims to reply to all communications as swiftly as possible.

Surgeries

An MP visits different areas in the constituency for an open advice clinic known as a surgery, usually

 Joanna Brown @joannabrownMP
Busy 2 hr surgery in Dalgeddie: issues incl unemployment, pensions, anti-social behaviour, plans for new airport & funding for university places #busybusy

 Joanna Brown @joannabrownMP
This morning from 9am on Radio Dalgeddie re tax of fatty foods. What do you think? Should unhealthy food be taxed more?

 Joanna Brown @joannabrownMP
@dalgeddieboy @bobtheplumber agreed that we need to look at boosting the economy and small businesses. I'll contact the business sec regarding his plans and get back to you.

 Joanna Brown @joannabrownMP
Fantastic day visiting Dalgeddie Primary. Pupils raised issues over the independence referendum, local sports facilities and cycling #futureMPs

 Joanna Brown @joannabrownMP
Managed to talk my way into presenting @ pupil's award ceremony @ Dalgeddie Primary

scheduled at a fixed time once a week. Constituents do not need to make an appointment and can drop in to the surgery to express concerns that they have directly to their MP. These concerns could be about local or national issues.

Figure 2.8 MPs have to juggle many competing demands!

What challenges exist for MPs?

The main role of MPs is to represent constituents. However, they have a whole series of different and conflicting pressures to contend with. MPs are also answerable to the political party they are attached to. They have to ensure that they have a good relationship with local and national media, and with local and national pressure groups. Added into this mix is trying to ensure a work–life balance in order to spend time with family and friends.

MPs often find that they cannot keep everyone happy and so they need to manage their decisions carefully, after considering all of these different demands.

Local constituents

MPs are voted in by their constituents and they have to represent their areas well. If they are judged not to have worked in the interests of their constituents, they might lose their job as people will vote for someone else at the next general election.

Political parties

Most MPs are attached to a political party. This means that they have been selected by the party and their campaign has been supported financially by the party. They will be expected to support party policies.

In addition, apart from a few exceptional circumstances, candidates know that many voters will vote for a political party regardless of the candidate. Indeed, many voters will not know who their candidates are but will vote for a political party to carry out the promises it makes in its manifesto. This means that MPs recognise that their political party has to have a big influence on the decisions they make at a local and national level.

Local political party

MPs have to ensure that they conduct their constituency business in line with the wishes of local party members. They have frequent meetings with local members to gauge the opinion of the party and decide what action to take. MPs recognise that as they approach the next general election it is the local members of their political party who will decide whether to keep them as a candidate.

FACT FILE

Party whips

Party whips can have a huge influence on an MP's decision making. If an MP faithfully follows what their party asks of them, they increase their chance of being promoted within the parliamentary party into a junior ministerial role, of being placed on key committees and even of becoming a key minister. In addition, as whips are appointed by the party leader, they are powerful figures who 'have the ear' of those in key positions. In a similar way, however, an MP who votes against the wishes of the whip and the party could find that the 'whip has been withdrawn' from them, which is effectively an expulsion from the party. This would severely affect their chance of re-election at the next general election.

At the beginning of each week, the whips send round a memorandum to MPs called 'The Whip', which highlights key votes taking place in the House of Commons. If an event is **underlined once**, it is considered acceptable should an MP not wish to attend; if **underlined twice**, an MP will only be allowed to be absent with a valid excuse; if **underlined three times**, an MP must attend.

Show your understanding

1. What factors influence MPs when they make decisions?
2. Why is representing constituents the most important role for an MP?
3. Give two reasons why an MP would want to be a member of a political party.
4. 'MPs know that the main reason they were elected was because of the party they are attached to.'
   To what extent do you agree with the above statement?
5. Explain the term 'following the party line'.
6. Read the Fact File on party whips.
   (a) In what ways could party whips be very influential in an MP's career path?
   (b) Explain how party whips communicate the wishes of the party.

National political party

When MPs are attending Parliament the political party has a lot of influence on their decision making. It is the party which often dictates what an MP does while in Parliament. In order to ensure that MPs carry out the wishes of the party they appoint **party whips**. This is sometimes referred to as **following the party line**. The whips are MPs who are selected by the party's leader to put pressure on their fellow party MPs to support the party in House of Commons voting and in the business done in Parliament.

Brown must decide

This week marks an important week for local MP Joanna Brown. Dalgeddie has been suffering due to the nationwide recession. Unemployment is on the rise and many families are finding life difficult as the cost of living continues to increase. Brown's political party is now in government and part of its manifesto was to increase the UK's air network. They are contemplating building a new airport in the Dalgeddie area.

Many constituents would welcome the introduction of an airport into the area.

The Transport Secretary estimates that up to 800 jobs would be created in the local area in construction and service jobs. This would halt the increasing unemployment in the area and provide a much-needed boost to the local economy as the airport would attract extra business into the area. Brown's party will be expecting her to fully support its proposals.

However, Brown also risks losing a lot of support as she has publicly supported constituents who have argued that Dalgeddie should be a protected area due to the recent award for the new wildlife sanctuary. In addition, local environmental pressure group Keep Dalgeddie Green has warned that if Brown breaks her word to support the local environment and instead backs the plan for a new airport, they will campaign against her.

Brown will be attending the public meeting which takes place on Thursday evening at 7p.m. in the Town Hall.

 Show your understanding

1 Read the newspaper article.
   (a) What national issues are affecting Dalgeddie?
   (b) What would be the estimated impact on employment of building the airport near to the town?
   (c) Why are some people against the building of the airport?

Branch out

2 Using the newspaper article on Joanna Brown's situation, in pairs, create a large table outlining the various conflicts, and their advantages and disadvantages for Joanna. You should set out your table like the one below. This first part is completed for you.

Decision	Advantages	Disadvantages
Support the airport	Constituents would be happy that new jobs will be created.	
Not support the airport		

The Houses of Parliament

The work of Parliament is carried out by both the House of Commons and the House of Lords. Both Houses are contained within the Palace of Westminster.

Both Houses carry out similar tasks: making new legislation, scrutinising the work of the government and debating relevant issues. The process of law-making by Parliament requires both Houses to look at detail, in order to debate and amend proposed laws, known as bills. In most cases, this process requires negotiation between the House of Commons and the House of Lords, thus creating laws which have been produced with careful thought. The House of Commons contains elected Members of Parliament and the House of Lords contains unelected peers known as Lords and Baronesses (see pages 52–58).

Why are laws created?

In the UK we do not have a written constitution. That is, we do not have a single document which lays down the basic rights and laws on which we base our society. Instead the UK has many laws which are constantly changing and evolving. Times change and, as a result, the UK Parliament must create new laws and amend existing ones. This process is called legislation. For example, after the terrorist attacks on

Which laws would you change?

- Change the age at which you can leave school?
- Increase the age at which you can drive?
- Lower the retirement age?

These ideas are all perfectly possible, but it will be mainly the government who will decide which laws need to be changed and it is the House of Commons and the House of Lords which will debate, discuss, amend and vote on new laws before they are passed to the monarch for Royal Assent.

London in 2005 and the attack on Glasgow Airport in 2007, the UK Parliament, led by the government, had to consider new ways of tackling terrorism and so introduced new laws. This legislation affects nearly everyone in the UK today, as security is now much tighter at transport hubs such as airports and at large public events such as music festivals.

How are laws created?

Creating or amending laws takes time and careful thought. The procedure of passing new legislation through Parliament is similar for both houses. A bill can be started in either House and it moves between both Houses on its way to becoming a law. Most laws are introduced by the government as a **White Paper**, which sets out what they are planning to put in the bill. Sometimes it can be introduced as a **Green Paper**, which sets out the proposed bill's ideas but asks for comments from the public. After this stage the proposed legislation becomes a **bill**, which essentially means that it is in the process of going through Parliament. If the bill manages to get through all the stages in Table 2.5, it receives Royal Assent and is made into an **Act**. This means that it is now law, or it will become law in the near future. This process ensures that all new laws are carefully considered.

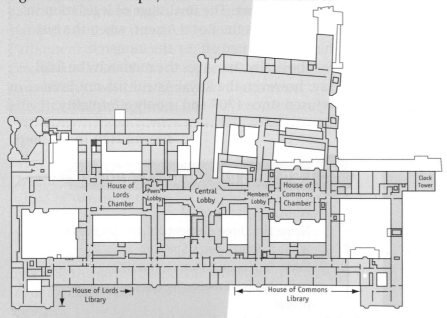

Figure 2.12 The House of Commons and the House of Lords are both part of the Palace of Westminster.

Show your understanding

1 What are the three main roles of each House?
2 Who works in each of the Houses of Parliament?
3 Look at the list of possible new laws, under 'Which laws would you change?' For each new law, give one possible advantage and one possible disadvantage of introducing it.
4 Give a definition for each of the following:
   (a) White Paper
   (b) Green Paper
   (c) Bill
   (d) Act.
5 Look at Table 2.5: in your own words, explain why you think it is important that new bills go through several stages before becoming Acts of Parliament.

What is the House of Commons?

The House of Commons is the elected body of Parliament and is where Members of Parliament (MPs) make decisions on how to run the country.

To be an MP, a person has to be elected in a constituency election by gaining more votes than any other candidate. At the 2010 general election there were 650 constituencies, and so there are 650 MPs in the House of Commons. Members of Parliament are elected by their constituents to make decisions on their behalf – this is known as representative democracy.

How does the House of Commons work?

The primary role of the House of Commons is to create new laws and amend old laws which help to run the country. It also scrutinises the government to ensure that its decisions are being checked.

In many ways the work of the House of Commons is similar to that of the House of Lords, but the main difference is that the House of Commons is an **elected chamber**. It acts as 'the voice of the people' and so has been given legitimacy by the UK public to lead the country and make decisions on its behalf. For this reason the House of Commons is known as the dominant chamber.

First Reading	A bill is first introduced in either the House of Commons or the House of Lords.
Second Reading	The bill is explained to the House, which then discusses and debates the principles of the bill.
Committee Stage	The House sets up a committee to go through the bill, line by line, until they produce an amended version of the bill to send back to the House.
Report Stage	The committee then produces a report and explains any amendments made. There is an opportunity for further amendments. A vote is usually taken at this stage before the bill is passed to the other House.
	The above processes are repeated in the opposite House.
Third Reading	When the process has been repeated, the House of Lords has an opportunity for a third reading and can suggest further amendments.
Royal Assent	If the bill has survived all of the stages and has been passed by both Houses in a vote known as a division, the Speaker of the House of Commons and the Lord Speaker announce that the bill has been given Royal Assent and has been made an Act of Parliament.

Table 2.5 The stages of a bill moving through the House of Commons and the House of Lords

Figure 2.13 The 650 constituencies of the UK by political party

Conservative

Labour

Liberal Democrat

Scottish National Party

Other

Shetland

Orkney

Central Scotland

Greater London

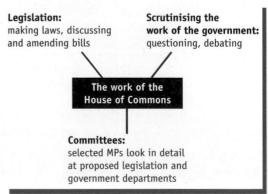

Legislation:
making laws, discussing and amending bills

Scrutinising the work of the government:
questioning, debating

The work of the House of Commons

Committees:
selected MPs look in detail at proposed legislation and government departments

Figure 2.14 The work of the House of Commons

What are the different roles in the House of Commons?

The House of Commons works on the principle of debate and therefore has an **adversarial** system. The members of the government which is in power sit on one side of the chamber and the members of the opposition sit opposite. Both sides present their arguments and then the whole chamber votes 'aye' or 'no' when the debate has finished.

Who have the most powerful roles in the House of Commons?

Prime minister

The prime minister is simply the leader of the governing party. In most cases this will be the party with the most seats in the House of Commons. Following the 2010 general election, David Cameron became prime minister, as he was the leader of the Conservatives. When David Cameron proposes new laws or measures he can, on most occasions, rely on Conservative MPs to back his plans. (This did not happen, however, with plans in 2012 to reform the House of Lords.) This is because of the party whip, which ensures that MPs obey the prime minister's wishes. The prime minister also has the power to appoint whoever he wants to the cabinet and this gives him **power of patronage**. MPs who have ambitions to gain a position in the cabinet need to give their party leader their full support. As the chairperson of the cabinet, the prime minister sets the agenda. Lastly, the prime minister is the face of the government. The public recognise the special position he or she holds and this gives the prime minister power over less well-known MPs.

Prime minister	The MP who is the leader of the ruling party becomes the prime minister. He or she is the head of the government.
Government	It sets the agenda in the House and introduces new legislation.
Cabinet	MPs from the ruling party who have responsibility for a government department make up the Cabinet.
Speaker	After a general election the chamber votes for an MP to become Speaker and he or she controls the debates.
Leader of the opposition	This is the MP who is leader of the second-largest party. He or she has more opportunity than the other party leaders to question the prime minister and criticise the government.
Shadow government or opposition	The second-largest party is known as the shadow government or opposition and it has more opportunity to question government ministers than the other minority parties.
Backbench MPs	Most MPs are backbenchers. They are MPs who are not government ministers or shadow government ministers.

Table 2.6 The different roles in the House of Commons

Cabinet

The cabinet is made up of MPs and peers selected by the prime minister to run government departments. Two of the most powerful positions are Chancellor of the Exchequer, who is in charge of government

Figure 2.15 David Cameron, Prime Minister

Figure 2.16 George Osborne MP, Chancellor of the Exchequer

Figure 2.17 William Hague MP, Foreign Secretary

Show your understanding

1 After the 2010 general election how many MPs were there in the UK?
2 In what way is the House of Commons democratic?
3 What are the three main roles of the House of Commons?
4 Why is the House of Commons an 'adversarial' system?
5 What is the role of the prime minister?
6 Explain how each of the following gives the prime minister political power:
   (a) party whip
   (b) patronage
   (c) collective responsibility.
7 Explain how the leader of the opposition can be influential.

finances and taxation, and Foreign Secretary, who represents the government abroad when dealing with issues such as conflicts and emergencies. Becoming a government minister will nearly double an MP's salary. All members of the cabinet need to publicly back the prime minister at all times, otherwise they can be removed or forced to resign from the cabinet. This is called **collective responsibility**.

Government

The prime minister selects MPs and peers to be part of the government. These MPs are usually those who have been most loyal to their party leader. Within the government is the cabinet, who are MPs in charge of specific government departments. In addition, there will be a number of junior ministers who help the government ministers run their departments.

Leader of the opposition

The leader of the opposition does not have any direct power in the House of Commons but is seen as the chief critic of the government. He or she has a high profile in the media and can have a big influence over the popularity of a government. For example, between 2008 and 2010, Prime Minister Gordon Brown often came under considerable pressure by the then Leader of the Opposition, David Cameron. This weakened his position in the eyes of the media and voters.

ICT task

Go to www.number10.gov.uk/the-coalition/the-cabinet/

Chose four cabinet ministers from the list and write notes on the following information about them using the links provided:

• their name and the department they are responsible for
• their responsibilities
• which constituency they represent
• background information about their life and work.

Case study: coalition government 2010

Following the 2010 general election, the UK government became a **coalition government**. This means that it is made up of more than one political party. This occurred because no party had an outright majority of seats.

Why is it important to have a majority?

For decades, the UK Parliament has been a **two-party system**. That is, it has been dominated by the Conservative Party or the Labour Party. On most occasions, one of the parties gains an overall majority of seats (over 50%) and rules as a **majority government**. This allows the party to carry out the promises made during the election campaign and in its manifesto. After all, it was voted in by the public because its plans were most attractive to voters. The party can be confident that any plans it has will gain the support of its own MPs and thus be passed in Parliament.

As you can see in Table 2.7, in 2010 the Conservatives did not manage to gain more than half of the seats in the House of Commons. As they gained the most seats with 307, they had the right to form a government,

Party	Seats	% of seats
Conservative	307	47.2
Labour	258	39.7
Liberal Democrat	57	8.8
Other MPs	28	4.3
Total	650	100

Table 2.7 General election result 2010

but on their own they would be a minority government. They would have had to rely on the support of MPs from other parties to get their legislation through and they might not have been able to carry out many of their manifesto promises.

Coalition agreement

After the 2010 general election, the Conservative Party entered into negotiation with the Liberal Democrats, and both parties announced that they would be working together in a coalition government. A new manifesto had to be drawn up which contained the plans of both parties. As a result, both parties had to make sacrifices over the promises they had made during the election campaign. Some would argue that this is unfair as no one voted for a partnership between parties and that the Liberal Democrats would have more influence over legislation than Labour despite only gaining 8.8% of the seats compared with Labour's 39.7%. Others might argue that coalition government increases the percentage of voters who voted for the government. The combined percentage of Conservative and Liberal Democrat voters is 56% – and so a majority of voters voted for the coalition parties.

Sacrifices made

Tuition fees

During the election campaign, the Conservatives promised to introduce an increase in tuition fees for students going to universities in England and Wales. During the election, the Liberal Democrats had promised not to increase tuition fees and in fact had signed a pledge not to do so. However, as part of the Coalition Agreement the Liberal Democrats supported an increase in tuition fees.

Electoral reform

During the election, the Liberal Democrats had promised to hold a referendum on changing the general election voting system from First Past The Post (FTPT) to the Single Transferable Vote (STV). The Conservatives had promised to maintain the FTPT system. Both parties negotiated and the Liberal Democrats had to drop demands for STV and instead had to settle for Alternative Vote (see page 17). As a result, during May 2011 there was a referendum on changing the voting system. The Conservatives campaigned against it and the Liberal Democrats campaigned for. The public overwhelmingly voted against change (see page 8).

Who is in control in the coalition government?

Ultimately, the prime minister is still in control of the cabinet. On the other hand, it could be argued that his position has been weakened as a result of forming a coalition. The Liberal Democrats have 5 and the Conservatives 18 government ministers. In nearly every government department there is a Liberal Democrat junior minister. After the general election in 2010, many Conservative MPs missed out on a position in government as space had to be made for their coalition partners. This weakened the prime minister's power. One example is David Mundell, who is MP for Dumfriesshire, Clydesdale and Tweeddale. He was Shadow Secretary of State for Scotland for a number of years before the 2010 election. He would have been in line to take up the position of Secretary of State for Scotland following a Conservative victory. After the creation of the coalition government, the position was given to Liberal Democrat Michael Moore, MP for Berwickshire, Roxburgh

Figure 2.18 May 2010: David Cameron and Nick Clegg launch the coalition and agree 'to put aside party differences and work hard for the national interest'.

and Selkirk. In addition, as the prime minister has to negotiate with Deputy Prime Minister Nick Clegg over new positions, his power of patronage has been slightly weakened.

Is the coalition government stable?

Since 2010, the government has introduced a number of far-reaching changes, including reform of the National Health Service in England and Wales, cuts to nearly all government departments, increases in tuition fees, and changes in social security. All of these have been backed by the coalition government. However, there are a number of issues which both parties clash over:

- **Europe** – the parties have opposing views on the UK's place within the European Union. Many Conservative MPs want a referendum on changing the UK's place in the EU, while the Liberal Democrats are traditionally pro-EU.

- **House of Lords Reform –** again the parties have opposing views. The Liberal Democrats promised to press forward with full reform of the House of Lords but many Conservative MPs want minimal change.

- **Changes to constituency boundaries –** David Cameron and his Conservative colleagues wish to change the number of constituencies from 650 to 600. This is seen as a vital change for the Conservatives in their search for a majority at the next election.

Due to the collapse of the House of Lords reform, the Liberal Democrats chose not to support a bill to change constituency boundaries. The headline in the *Herald* newspaper of 7 August declared: 'Coalition meltdown after Clegg gives up over Lords: deputy PM orders party's MPs to block Tory reforms.' In January 2013 the Liberal Democrats voted with Labour to defeat the bill to change constituency boundaries.

Figure 2.19 Liberal Democrat leader Nick Clegg with his election pledge on tuition fees. The Liberal Democrats chose to support the Conservatives in voting for an increase.

→ Added value

You could provide a detailed report on the successes and failures of the coalition government. To help enhance your report you may wish to carry out a survey in your local area.

Show your understanding

1 Define the term 'coalition government'.
2 Why is it considered important to have a majority in Parliament?
3 Why do some people believe that forming a coalition government is unfair?
4 In what ways have sacrifices been made by both the Conservatives and the Liberal Democrats?
5 'The prime minister's position has been weakened as a result of forming a coalition with the Liberal Democrats.'
   To what extent do you agree with the above statement?

The House of Lords

What is the House of Lords?

The House of Lords works in partnership with the House of Commons in helping to shape new laws, and it also helps to scrutinise the work of the government. The House of Lords is also known as the upper house or advisory chamber, and it is situated within the Palace of Westminster, opposite the House of Commons. Within the House of Lords there are peers, known as lords or baronesses. Unlike the House of Commons, these peers are unelected by the public. Lords and baronesses do not receive a salary but are given a tax-free allowance of around £300 per day for attending Parliament or carrying out other duties.

How do you become a member of the House of Lords?

Historically, the majority of members in the House of Lords were hereditary peers who had a right to their title by birth, and their titles were passed down through generations of families

Figure 2.20 The House of Lords chamber

> **What you will learn:**
>
> 1 The purpose and functions of the House of Lords.
> 2 The different types of members in the House of Lords.
> 3 The powers of the House of Lords.
> 4 Proposed reforms to the House of Lords.

who were predominantly rich landowners or from the upper classes. However, following various reforms, the House of Lords now consists of mainly appointed peers. There are very few limitations on who can become a peer. A lord or baroness must:

- be over 21 years old
- be a citizen of the United Kingdom, the Commonwealth or Ireland
- have expertise or many years of experience in their field.

Today there are two main types of peers.

Lords temporal

The majority of peers in the House of Lords are **life peers**, who have been awarded the position by the government and Parliament. The government can nominate individuals for a peerage and these are then reviewed by the Appointments Commission. The Appointments Commission was set up in 2000 and its role is to make recommendations for peers to the reigning monarch. In 2012 there were 711 life peers in the House of Lords. These peers were given the unofficial title of 'the people's peers' and it was hoped that they would help modernise the House of Lords to reflect UK society. The Lords temporal are individuals from all walks of life. Among the life peers there are former politicians, successful business people, distinguished scientists, renowned artists and even successful athletes. Their title is awarded for life but cannot be passed on to their family and so it dies with them.

There are a number of **hereditary peers** still present in the House of Lords. However, following the House of Lords Act 1999, it was decided that these peers would gradually be replaced by lords

Area	Number	% of Lords
Politics	151	22
Business and commerce	61	9
Banking and finance	59	8
Education	59	8
Religion	29	4
Journalism and media	25	4
Medicine and health care	15	2
Armed forces	12	2
Police	8	1
Engineering	5	1

Table 2.8 Selected professional backgrounds of life peers

Figure 2.21 Former Deputy Prime Minister John Prescott was awarded a peerage in recognition of his many years of service to politics.

and baronesses whose peerages cannot be passed down through families. This change has resulted in the number of hereditary peers dropping from 63% in 1996 to 13% in 2000, and a continued fall to 11% (89 hereditary peers) in 2012. This number will continue to decline until there are none.

Life peers and hereditary peers can be members of a political party but many remain independent. This results in there being less of an emphasis on party loyalty in the House of Lords.

Lords spiritual

In the House of Lords there are also peers known as the Lords spiritual, who are there because of their positions in the Church of England. They may only sit in the House of Lords while they hold these church positions, and are all either bishops or archbishops. In 2012 there were 26 Lords spiritual.

Some well-known peers

There are many famous life peers who enjoy wide recognition by the public.

Lord Sugar

Lord Coe

Figure 2.22 Alan Sugar, a highly successful businessman and the face of the popular TV show *The Apprentice*

Figure 2.23 Sebastian Coe, Olympic gold medallist and chairman of the 2012 London Olympics

In what ways is the House of Lords different from the House of Commons?

Members of the House of Lords are not elected by the public so their role in Parliament is mainly advisory. They are not involved in running the country on a day-to-day basis but they can influence the law-making process.

Show your understanding

1 What are the conditions for membership of the House of Lords?
2 What is the main role of the House of Lords?
3 Historically, how did people become a member of the House of Lords?
4 Explain the difference between life peers and hereditary peers.
5 How many life peers were in the House of Lords in 2012?
6 What effect has the House of Lords Act 1999 had on the types of peers in the House of Lords?

Develop your skills

7 'The people's peers reflect UK society. Their background is mainly in the healthcare and education sectors.' (*Hashim Khan*)

Using Table 2.8, explain why Hashim Khan could be accused of exaggeration.

What is the power of the House of Lords?

It plays a key role in the passing of legislation

Proposed laws, known as bills, are created by Parliament, which are then debated by both the House of Commons and the House of Lords. All bills usually pass through the House of Lords before becoming new legislation. However, the powers of the Lords are limited as they cannot reject a bill relating to fiscal matters (taxation) and they can only delay all other bills by one year. The House of Lords, therefore, cannot stop a bill outright, but it can cause a delay that might result in the bill being changed or even dropped entirely by the government.

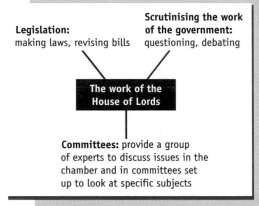

Figure 2.24 The work of the House of Lords

House of Commons	House of Lords
MPs are elected.	Peers are appointed.
MPs can be from any background and have any qualifications.	Most peers are appointed due to their expertise or experience in a specific field.
MPs have to win an election every four to five years.	Once appointed, lords and baronesses have the position for life.
MPs are paid a salary and expenses.	Peers only receive an allowance and expenses.
MPs represent constituencies.	Peers only represent themselves.
Nearly all MPs are members of a political party.	Many peers are members of a political party but a large number are not.
Only elected MPs can sit in the House of Commons.	In the House of Lords there are life peers, hereditary peers and Church of England bishops.

Table 2.9 Differences between the House of Commons and House of Lords

Salisbury Convention

Under the Parliament Act the power of the House of Lords is limited. Ultimately defeats in the House of Lords can be overturned in the House of Commons under the Salisbury Convention, which limits the power of peers if a government does not have a majority in the House of Lords. In addition, the House of Lords cannot delay legislation which forms part of the government's key bills which were promised as part of its election manifesto. This is because the public voted for those policies in the election and it would be undemocratic for unelected peers to interfere with the wishes of the electorate.

As the House of Lords is predominantly made up of life peers who have vast experience in specific areas, the movement of a bill through the House of Lords allows it to be considered by those who have acute knowledge of the issue. This helps Parliament to take a responsible approach to creating new legislation. In addition, the sheer volume of work the House of Commons has to get through can at times result in proposed laws being rushed, so the House of Lords allows more time to be dedicated to these bills.

It scrutinises the government

Debates

Just like the House of Commons, the House of Lords also has a full programme of debates in its chamber. The level of debate is regarded as being of a very high quality, as experienced professionals can offer their wisdom and guidance on issues. In addition, the debates are much calmer than those

Figure 2.25 Members of the House of Lords in the ceremonial costume they wear for the state opening of Parliament

which take place in the House of Commons, as political parties do not have as much influence in the House of Lords and so debates are usually less confrontational. The peers will debate on important issues which affect the nation such as health care, education, terrorism, immigration and justice.

Case study: House of Lords – Counter-Terrorism Act 2008

In October 2008, the Labour government proposed that changes should be made to the limit on time for holding suspected terrorists in police custody. They proposed holding suspects for a maximum of 42 days, which meant a 14-day increase from the existing rule. After narrowly passing through the House of Commons, the bill was defeated in the House of Lords by 309 votes to 118. As the Salisbury Convention did not apply to the government at that time (due to a Labour majority in the House of Lords), the government had to leave out the increase in detention from the bill. The remaining parts of the bill were made an Act of Parliament.

Case study: House of Lords – Welfare Reform Act 2012

The coalition agreement between the Conservatives and Liberal Democrats after the 2010 general election stated that there were to be wide-ranging reforms to the UK's welfare system. After the bill had been considered by both Houses, it was given Royal Assent in March 2012 and was made law. This happened despite the House of Lords expressing major concerns over various parts of the new legislation. In fact, the House of Lords voted down the decision to include Child Benefit in the calculations of the household benefits cap of £26,000. The Lords argued that the move would unfairly punish households with larger families. Despite the Lords voting against the government, the House of Commons overturned the Lords vote and the bill was passed.

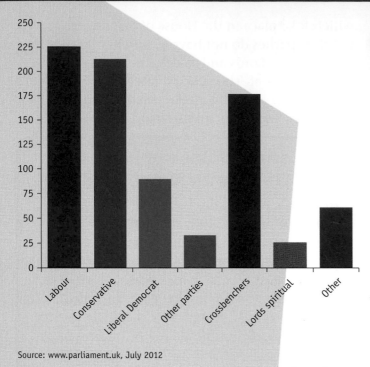

Source: www.parliament.uk, July 2012

Figure 2.26 Party membership of the House of Lords

Committees

The Lords also form expert committees who will unpick bills and thoroughly address any issues. The main role of these committees is to scrutinise the government's plans for legislation. It could be argued that because many peers are top scientists, lawyers, business people and so on, they will assess the merits of a proposed law more effectively than MPs. Committees from the Lords are seen as being effective as they are less affected by 'party politics' than House of Commons committees. That is, peers are not as influenced by the party whip.

It is seen as being more independent

Although the majority of peers do belong to a political party, they are not as tied to the party as their colleagues in the House of Commons. They have freedom from elections which weakens the party whip's impact on their decision making, and so they are seen as being independent. Also, many members are not members of any political party; they are known as **crossbenchers**, and can carry out their tasks as independent thinkers. Figure 2.26 shows the political membership of the House of Lords.

Figure 2.27 Former Scottish First Minister Jack McConnell became a life peer in June 2010. His official title is Baron McConnell of Glenscorrodale.

Reform of the House of Lords

Why is the House of Lords a controversial issue?

The House of Lords is part of Parliament, which decides how the UK is managed and run. This is controversial as peers in the House of Lords are unelected. They are not answerable to the people and they are in position for life. Many would argue that the House of Lords has no place in a modern, democratic political system.

House of Lords Act 1999

The Labour Party, under Prime Minister Tony Blair, removed all but 92 of the House of Lords hereditary peers. In July 2012 the number had fallen to 89. After this change a commission (a group of selected experts) was set up in 2000, headed by Lord Wakeham. The commission looked at completely reforming the Lords. Since this time, successive governments have promised to make changes to the House of Lords but have largely failed. The only major reform to take place has been the movement of the Court of Appeal from the Lords to the UK Supreme Court in 2009.

House of Lords Reform Bill 2012

The coalition agreement following the 2010 general election included reform of the House of Lords and in June 2012 the government produced a bill recommending the following reforms:

- The number of peers would be reduced from 826 members to 450.
- The majority (80%) of members would be elected.
- 90 members (20%) would still be appointed, by an Appointments Commission, on a non-party basis.
- Time-limits – peers would serve a non-renewable 15-year term instead of being members for life.
- A reduced number of bishops – the number of Church of England bishops would be reduced.

Why has reform been so problematic?

- MPs feel that if peers were to be elected to the House of Lords this would reduce their own power and the House of Lords would no longer be only a 'revising chamber'.
- Since the reduction in the number of hereditary peers, many believe that the House of Lords has become more effective.
- An elected second chamber would remove the relative independence of the House of Lords and would see peers hustling for votes and following the **party line**.
- Many people feel that the time and resources used in trying to reform the House of Lords would be better used in trying to improve the lives of the British public, for example, by tackling unemployment or improving living conditions.

- The chamber would still be called the House of Lords but members would not have the title 'Lord'. A new title was to be decided upon.

As we have seen, it became clear in August 2012 that Prime Minister David Cameron would not be able to persuade the Conservative backbenchers to accept the reform. Nick Clegg recognised this reality and announced that reform of House of Lords would not be achieved.

→ Added value

You could create a short film on the arguments for and against reform of the House of Lords, in which you interview classmates and your family, and even arrange an interview with a peer.

Arguments for and against reform of the House of Lords

FOR

The Church of England has no place in politics and does not reflect a modern, multicultural Britain.

The costs of the House of Lords are due to increase as more peers are created. This is a waste of money.

The Lords have real power but cannot be held responsible by voters.

The way peers are appointed is unfair and could be open to allegations of sleaze.

AGAINST

It is important that we use the most experienced people to help run our country and help make important decisions.

We should preserve our national heritage, as the House of Lords is part of our culture and history.

The House of Lords is important because they look after our long-term interests and are not worried about elections.

The government should spend its time on improving the economy or health service rather than dealing with constitutional reform.

Show your understanding

1. Why do some people believe the House of Lords should not be part of a modern, democratic political system?
2. What changes did the Labour government of 1997–2001 make to the set-up of the House of Lords?
3. Select two reasons why reforming the House of Lords has been so problematic and explain why you feel these are the most influential reasons.
4. To what extent would the proposals set forward in the House of Lords Reform Bill 2012 make membership of the House of Lords more democratic?

ICT task

In pairs, create an 8–10 slide presentation detailing the arguments you find most convincing about reform of the House of Lords. Your presentation must contain an introduction, three arguments for, three arguments against, and an overall conclusion.

Political parties in the UK

What is a political party?

In the UK there are three main political parties: the Conservative, Labour and Liberal Democrat parties. These three parties make up most of the MPs in the House of Commons and most of the peers in the House of Lords. There are a number of smaller political parties which play a part in politics in the UK; however, these three parties have the most influence in UK politics.

A political party is an organisation of people who have similar political beliefs and opinions. They are organisations which aim to have representation within Parliament and so hope to influence how the country is run. Traditionally, in the UK we have what is known as a two-party system of politics, as our elections have been dominated by the Conservative Party and the Labour Party. However, since 2010 we have had a government which has combined Conservative and Liberal Democrat MPs. When two parties share power, this is known as a coalition government. In the 2010 election, there were 650 available seats. The more seats a political party gains by their candidates winning in constituencies and becoming MPs, the more influence it can exert over the running of the country. The leader of the party with the most seats in the UK becomes the prime minister.

Political parties continuously try to win support among the general public so that when an election comes round they have a good chance of achieving votes. This can be very expensive and this is one reason why most MPs are members of a political party rather than independents.

It is very important to political parties that they have a positive public image and a likeable party leader. If the public do not like a party leader, support for the party will drop. In the 2010 election, the Labour Party suffered heavy losses at the hands of the Conservatives. Many people attributed this loss to the party leader, Gordon Brown, whose public image was less than favourable.

What is the difference between the political parties?

Political parties have their own visions and plans for how they think the country should be run. These plans can be listed under key **policy** areas such as education, environment, justice, economy and health. Before an election, each political party publishes a document outlining its policies, known as a **party manifesto**. If an MP from a party wins a seat, the party members will expect him or her to help in ensuring the party's policies are promoted, even if this conflicts with the needs of the MP's constituents. The Fact File on each political party tells you a little about each party and some of the policies they believe will make the UK a better country.

FACT FILE

The Conservative Party

About

The Conservative Party, sometimes referred to as the Tory Party or the Tories, is the largest party in the UK. In the 2010 general election it gained 307 seats, which enabled it to form a government and its leader David Cameron to become prime minister. As it did not gain a clear majority of the seats available, it formed a coalition government with the Liberal Democrats. This was the first time since 1997 that the UK had a Conservative prime minister. The Conservatives generally have support from southern England and have their largest support from the middle and upper classes. They do not tend to gain much support in working-class areas. As they have formed part of the government, many of their policies have become a reality.

Key policies

- Aim to reduce the UK's budget deficit drastically within five years, thus clearing the national debt.
- Create the 'Big Society' – allow charities, voluntary groups and cooperatives to set up new Academy schools, independent of local authority control, and to run other public services.
- Develop a high-speed rail network connecting cities in England, Scotland and Wales, with construction to begin in 2015.
- Introduce greater private business involvement into the National Health Service in England and Wales to improve efficiency.
- Commit to replacing Trident to maintain the UK's nuclear deterrent.

Figure 2.29 The Conservative Party logo

Figure 2.28 David Cameron

FACT FILE

The Labour Party

About

The Labour Party is led by Ed Miliband MP. In the 2010 general election it gained 258 seats, making it the second-largest party in the House of Commons. This means that it is the **opposition party**. It plays a key role in scrutinising the government. The Labour Party had a majority government in the UK from 1997 to 2010. Traditionally it gains most of its support from the north of England, Scotland and Wales, and has its largest support from the working classes. The party has strong links to trade unions, who influence many of their policies.

Key policies

- Reduce the UK's budget deficit but protect frontline services such as the National Health Service, schools and policing.

- Create employment or training for those out of work for six months or more.

- Guarantee cancer patients will see a specialist within two weeks of diagnosis and get test results within one week.

- Cut greenhouse gas emissions by 34% by 2020.

- Commit to replacing Trident to maintain the UK's nuclear deterrent.

Labour

Figure 2.31 The Labour Party logo

Figure 2.30 Ed Miliband

FACT FILE

The Liberal Democrats

About

Nick Clegg MP is Leader of the Liberal Democrats and is currently deputy prime minister, as the party formed a coalition government with the Conservatives after the 2010 general election. Before this event, the Liberal Democrats found themselves on the fringes of decision making in the House of Commons as the Conservatives and Labour have dominated UK politics for decades. Since becoming part of the government, the Liberal Democrats have found that their support has fallen in other elections as they have had to make some unpopular decisions to get the UK out of the worst economic situation since the Great Depression. As they are part of the coalition government, they saw 75% of their manifesto implemented in the Coalition Agreement.

Key policies

- Restore the UK economy by reducing the deficit and building a sustainable economy that is not reliant on the banks in the City of London but creates jobs across the country, especially green jobs.

- Provide £2.5 billion per year for a 'Pupil Premium' for schools in England to give the poorest pupils extra support.

- Raise the point at which people start paying tax on their incomes to £10,000, which means millions of taxpayers get a tax cut.

- Reform the voting system to end First Past The Post in the general elections and make the House of Lords elected.

- Reduce the UK nuclear arms stocks and kick-start global disarmament.

Figure 2.33 The Liberal Democrat Party logo

Figure 2.32 Nick Clegg

Show your understanding

1 What is a political party?
2 Name the three main political parties in the UK.
3 Why was the 2010 UK general election particularly important for the Liberal Democrats?
4 Why is it important that a party has a likeable leader?
5 Apart from having a strong leader, how else do parties gain the support of the public?
6 Study the Fact Files about the political parties.
 (a) Who are the leaders of the three main political parties?
 (b) Which parties are currently in power in the UK?
 (c) How many seats did each party win in the 2010 UK general election?

Branch out
7 Look at the policies of each political party. If you were able to vote, which party would you vote for? Justify your decision by referring to at least two policies.

Participation in UK politics

Voting in an election is not the only way people can take part in politics in the UK. People who support a political party can get actively involved with that party by joining as a **party member**.

How do you become a member of a political party?

Becoming a member of a political party is easy. Many people feel a connection to a political party's beliefs and join by paying an annual membership fee or a donation. Anyone can become a member of a political party. They can then attend local party meetings, discuss issues on the party blog websites and even attend the UK national conferences. Political parties are democratic organisations and it is the local members who decide on who stands as a candidate for each seat.

A party member usually gets involved in campaigning at election time by trying to convince constituents to vote for their party's candidate. This campaigning may involve handing out leaflets,

putting up posters, canvassing or even trying to drum up support on social media websites like Twitter or Facebook (see page 11).

How do you become a candidate in an election?

In working hard for your political party you may decide that you want to stand as a **candidate** for election yourself. First you would need to be elected by the local party members and then, once chosen as a party candidate, you would compete against candidates from other parties and independent candidates. You could stand to be elected as a local councillor or even as an MSP or MP.

A person would have to have certain personal qualities to stand for election such as:

Figure 2.34 Personal qualities of a political candidate

Show your understanding

1 What influence does a person have in a political party when they join as a member?
2 Describe the various methods of campaigning that a party member can be involved in at election time.
3 How do you become a political party's candidate for an election?
4 Study the various personal qualities required to stand as a candidate for a political party. Pick three that you feel are the most important. Explain your choices.

Branch out
5 In pairs, select at least six personal qualities and create a job advertisement or leaflet for Jobcentre Plus. Your advertisement should explain why a candidate and an MP would need each of the six personal qualities.

The work of an MSP

What is a Member of the Scottish Parliament?

Members of the Scottish Parliament (MSPs) are elected by the people of Scotland to represent them in the Scottish Parliament. They make decisions that shape our country and work to better the lives of their constituents. Each of the 129 MSPs represents a particular area of the country: either a **constituency** or a **region**. There are 73 MSPs each representing a constituency and 56 representing the eight regions of Scotland (seven MSPs in each region).

Once elected, MSPs serve their constituents for four years until the next election. In that time they split their work between working in their constituency or region and working at Parliament in Edinburgh. MSPs receive an annual salary of £57,521 plus expenses for travel and accommodation.

What you will learn:

1 The role of MSPs in Parliament.
2 The role of MSPs in the constituency.
3 What challenges exist for MSPs.
4 How women and ethnic minorities are represented in the Scottish Parliament.

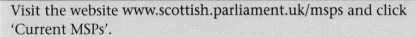

ICT task

Visit the website www.scottish.parliament.uk/msps and click 'Current MSPs'.

Find the MSP who represents you and your constituency, then click on the link to his or her profile.

1 From the profile page, complete the following tasks:
   a Which political party does your MSP belong to?
   b Which committees does your MSP belong to?
   c Under 'Parliamentary Activities', click the 'Recent Questions' tab. List the three most recent questions your MSP has asked in Parliament.
2 Pick any other three MSPs and do the same research for them. Do any of the MSPs ask specific questions relating to their constituencies?
3 Name the MSP(s) who represent the following:
   a Rutherglen constituency
   b Moray constituency
   c Highlands and Islands region (seven MSPs).
4 How many MSPs are men and how many are women?

Branch out

5 Visit the website of Paul Martin MSP – www.paulmartinmsp.org.uk. Create a profile for Paul Martin and investigate some of the work he is carrying out as an MSP.

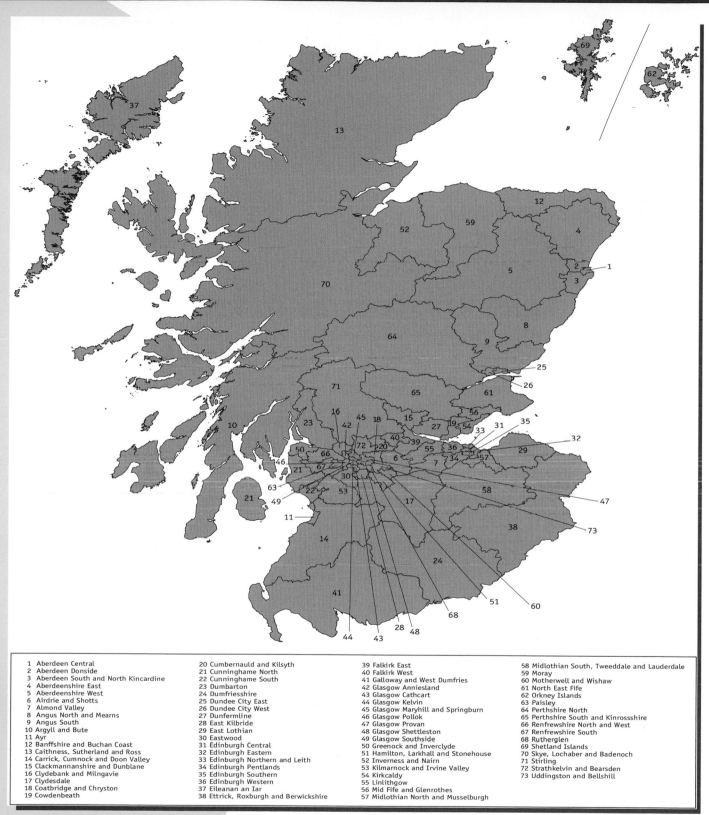

Figure 3.1 The 73 constituencies of Scotland

1 Aberdeen Central
2 Aberdeen Donside
3 Aberdeen South and North Kincardine
4 Aberdeenshire East
5 Aberdeenshire West
6 Airdrie and Shotts
7 Almond Valley
8 Angus North and Mearns
9 Angus South
10 Argyll and Bute
11 Ayr
12 Banffshire and Buchan Coast
13 Caithness, Sutherland and Ross
14 Carrick, Cumnock and Doon Valley
15 Clackmannanshire and Dunblane
16 Clydebank and Milngavie
17 Clydesdale
18 Coatbridge and Chryston
19 Cowdenbeath

20 Cumbernauld and Kilsyth
21 Cunninghame North
22 Cunninghame South
23 Dumbarton
24 Dumfriesshire
25 Dundee City East
26 Dundee City West
27 Dunfermline
28 East Kilbride
29 East Lothian
30 Eastwood
31 Edinburgh Central
32 Edinburgh Eastern
33 Edinburgh Northern and Leith
34 Edinburgh Pentlands
35 Edinburgh Southern
36 Edinburgh Western
37 Eileanan an Iar
38 Ettrick, Roxburgh and Berwickshire

39 Falkirk East
40 Falkirk West
41 Galloway and West Dumfries
42 Glasgow Anniesland
43 Glasgow Cathcart
44 Glasgow Kelvin
45 Glasgow Maryhill and Springburn
46 Glasgow Pollok
47 Glasgow Provan
48 Glasgow Shettleston
49 Glasgow Southside
50 Greenock and Inverclyde
51 Hamilton, Larkhall and Stonehouse
52 Inverness and Nairn
53 Kilmarnock and Irvine Valley
54 Kirkcaldy
55 Linlithgow
56 Mid Fife and Glenrothes
57 Midlothian North and Musselburgh

58 Midlothian South, Tweeddale and Lauderdale
59 Moray
60 Motherwell and Wishaw
61 North East Fife
62 Orkney Islands
63 Paisley
64 Perthshire North
65 Perthshire South and Kinrossshire
66 Renfrewshire North and West
67 Renfrewshire South
68 Rutherglen
69 Shetland Islands
70 Skye, Lochaber and Badenoch
71 Stirling
72 Strathkelvin and Bearsden
73 Uddingston and Bellshill

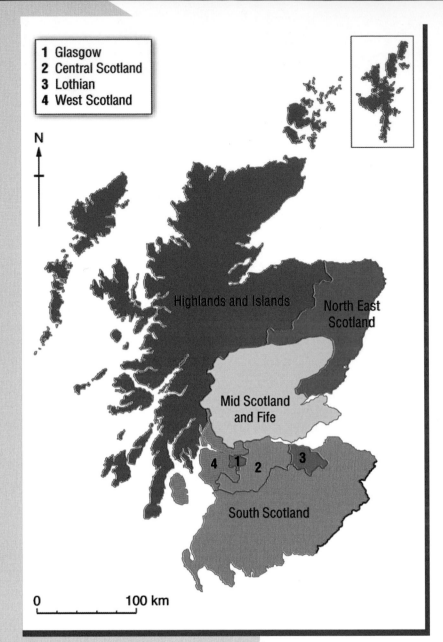

1 Glasgow
2 Central Scotland
3 Lothian
4 West Scotland

N

Highlands and Islands

North East Scotland

Mid Scotland and Fife

4 1 2 3

South Scotland

0   100 km

Figure 3.2 The eight regions of Scotland

What does an MSP do?

Put simply, an MSP's job is to represent their constituents, whether they voted for them or not. We live in a representative democracy, which means that MSPs act as representatives of the general public. They act as the 'voice' of the people and they make decisions on our behalf.

When in Parliament, MSPs carry out these duties by debating and voting on proposed laws, asking questions of the government and also sitting on committees which will report on certain issues such as the economy or the environment. Within the constituency, MSPs will work hard to ensure they are meeting the demands of their constituents, dealing with any problems or issues that the constituency is facing and generally working to make the community a better place to live.

MSPs usually work in their constituency on Mondays and Fridays, with weekend work optional. Many MSPs will spend some of their weekend working. Tuesday to Thursday is spent at Parliament in Edinburgh (see page 71).

Andy Stenhouse MSP

After the Scottish Parliament election, Andy Stenhouse was elected to serve Havenside constituency as its Member of the Scottish Parliament. Until the next Scottish Parliament election in four years' time, his full-time job will be to represent his constituents in a number of ways, both in the constituency and in Parliament. He needs to be willing to help individual constituents and local groups who have problems or concerns within the constituency. They may also have concerns about wider issues such as the Scottish economy or issues about taxation.

Andy Stenhouse must ensure that he commits enough time to helping his constituents – he faces the prospect of losing his seat (and thus his job) if his constituents decide he has not been successful in his role.

DIARY OF ANDY STENHOUSE MSP

Work in the constituency and Parliament

Sunday

CONSTITUENCY	Morning	Catch up and review the Sunday papers.
	Afternoon	Relax with the family – visit to local park.
	Evening	Family time.

Monday

CONSTITUENCY	Morning	Head into the constituency office. Plan the week ahead, finalise diary and schedule with office staff.
	Afternoon	Catch up with letters and emails received over the weekend. Reply to as many constituents as possible. Visit local primary school to present at the prize giving ceremony.
	Evening	Attend town meeting about possibility of new golf resort in Havenside. Read committee papers and prepare for Parliament on Tuesday.

Tuesday

PARLIAMENT	Morning	Travel to Parliament (Edinburgh) by train.
	Afternoon	Chair the Welfare Reform Committee meeting. Meet a group of schoolchildren from my constituency who are on a school trip for a tour of Parliament.
	Evening	Meet with fellow party MSPs to discuss proposal of a new bill.

Wednesday

PARLIAMENT	Morning	Sit on cross-party Fair Trade Committee to debate farming in developing countries.
	Afternoon	Attend a debate in the chamber about the possibility of a new golf resort in my constituency.
	Evening	Prepare for First Minister's Questions tomorrow.

Thursday

PARLIAMENT	Morning	Meet with pressure group representatives from Havenside Green Alliance.
	Afternoon	Attend General Question Time. Attend First Minister's Questions in the chamber. Ask about government plans to tackle unemployment in my constituency.
	Evening	Travel home to constituency by train.

Friday

CONSTITUENCY	Morning	Hold surgery in community centre at 10a.m. Meet with neighbourhood watch group to discuss antisocial behaviour.
	Afternoon	Interview with local newspaper and radio appearance at 4p.m.
	Evening	Attend charity dinner – make speech congratulating charity on good work.

Saturday

CONSTITUENCY	Morning	Attend monthly farmers' market and mingle with local constituents.
	Afternoon	Visit the new football stadium of Havenside FC and meet fans.
	Evening	Family time.

Show your understanding

1 How are MSPs elected and for how long are they in the position?
2 What is the annual salary of an MSP?
3 Describe how an MSP's working week is split between constituency and Parliament.
4 Study the diary of Andy Stenhouse MSP.
   (a) List three things Andy is doing to help his constituents.
   (b) In Parliament, what Committee is Andy the chair of?
   (c) Overall, do you think MSPs get enough free time? Justify your answer.

Figure 3.3 The Scottish Parliament building

What types of tasks do MSPs complete in Parliament?

MSPs have a large number of commitments when they are in Parliament. There are some tasks that are a compulsory part of the job of an MSP but many are at the MSP's own discretion. This allows MSPs to concentrate on the specific issues affecting their constituents and also issues which they themselves have an interest in.

Motions and debates

As well as debating proposals for any new bills (laws), an MSP can put forward a **motion**. A motion is a proposal for the Parliament to do something or express an opinion about an issue, and it is the most common means by which MSPs initiate debates within the Parliament chamber.

Motions can be about local, national or even international issues that affect Scotland. For example, in 2012 Jamie Hepburn MSP proposed a motion that was accepted for debate. The motion was about the need for an International Arms Trade Treaty, as he believed that Scotland, as a member (through the UK) of the United Nations, should help prevent weapons being sold to the wrong people, especially in developing countries. The debate was worthwhile in bringing a consensus among all MSPs that Scotland should back a new arms treaty. The First Minister stated, 'The Scottish Government is strongly supportive of an international arms trade treaty.'

Question Time

Every Thursday morning MSPs participate in **General Question Time**. This is when MSPs get the opportunity to question a government minister about his or her department. Government ministers are MSPs who are chosen by the First Minister to manage a government department, and key departments such as Health and Education have their own government ministers. Every week ministers have to answer questions put forward by MSPs. This allows MSPs to scrutinise decisions that ministers have made. There are strict rules over the submission of questions and most are 'seen' beforehand to allow the minister to prepare an answer. MSPs can also ask government ministers **written questions**, to which the minister has to respond within ten days. Asking questions is a very useful tool for MSPs to highlight specific problems faced by their constituency and possibly find a solution from the Scottish Government.

Every Thursday at noon, after General Question Time, is **First Minister's Question Time**. This gives the leaders of the other parties and some MSPs an opportunity to ask the head of the Scottish government questions directly. During a 30-minute period, First Minister Alex Salmond has to answer 'seen' questions and justify his government's stance on various issues. First Minister's Question Time can get quite lively, with opposition MSPs wanting to 'catch out' the First Minister and perhaps make him struggle under questioning.

Figure 3.4 The Scottish Parliament debating chamber

FACT FILE

Examples of questions asked at First Minister's Question Time

- To ask the First Minister whether the Scottish Government will provide additional funding to community projects to reduce reoffending by criminals.

- To ask the First Minister what steps the Scottish Government is taking to promote Scottish business overseas.

- To ask the First Minister what measures the Scottish Government is taking to tackle female unemployment in light of concerns that women are being disproportionately affected by job losses.

Committees

Most MSPs are members of at least one committee. A committee works to scrutinise government proposals and may conduct inquiries into specific matters. Each committee is given a particular area or subject to examine in detail. For example, the Education and Culture Committee considers and reports on matters relating to school and pre-school education as well as culture and the arts.

There are fifteen different committees with most having between seven and nine MSPs as members. Each committee will also have a convener and a deputy convener to chair the meetings. Membership and convenership have to reflect the balance of political power in the Parliament as a whole. Committees can introduce new bills (laws). Since the 2011 election the SNP has had a majority in each of the committees. Opposition parties claim that this weakens the ability of the committees to scrutinise SNP government policies.

MSPs also have the power to attempt to introduce new bills. The majority of members' bills are not successful – only 7 out of 29 bills received Royal Assent in the last session of the Scottish Parliament (2007–11). See page 84 for information about other types of bills.

Voting

At the end of days when the Parliament sits, MSPs can vote at '**Decision Time**'. This is usually held at 5p.m. with MSPs voting on any business that has passed through Parliament that day. Generally the result of most votes can be predicted beforehand since political parties normally instruct their MSPs which way to vote through the whip system (see page 76). The Scottish Parliament is fortunate to have an electronic voting system in the chamber, which means MSPs simply push a button to cast their vote. Consequently, results are known within seconds.

Case study: Scrutinising policy – the Justice Committee

About

The Justice Committee meets every Tuesday morning. Its primary role is to scrutinise the policies and performance of the Scottish Government and its agencies in matters related to justice. Christine Grahame, MSP for Midlothian South, Tweeddale and Lauderdale, is convener of the committee. The committee can also carry out fact-finding visits around Scotland to find out more about the justice system in practice.

Example of work

The Justice Committee spent a large part of 2012 scrutinising a bill proposed by the Scottish Government to reform the police and fire service. The Police and Fire Reform (Scotland) Bill aimed to create a single police service and a single fire and rescue service for the whole of Scotland. After much scrutiny, the committee agreed the bill in principle, and the next stage of progress could then be made. Committee convener Christine Grahame MSP said, 'Our role in scrutinising this bill was to make sure that the new national police and fire and rescue forces can actually deliver the services effectively throughout Scotland. The overwhelming majority of the committee believed they can.'

Case study: Conducting inquiries – Economy, Energy and Tourism

About

The Economy, Energy and Tourism Committee meetings are generally held on Wednesday mornings. The committee's key roles are to scrutinise government policy and to conduct inquiries into matters relating to the economy, energy and tourism. Murdo Fraser, MSP for Mid-Scotland and Fife, is the convener of the committee.

Example of work

In 2012 the committee conducted an inquiry into the Scottish Government's green energy targets. In doing so they called witnesses and went on fact-finding visits to investigate the achievability of the Scottish Government's 2020 renewable energy targets, the merits of the targets and what the risks and barriers are to realising them. One witness the committee called was Donald Trump, the American billionaire. They wanted to find out his views on and wider concerns regarding the impact of wind farms on tourism and the economy in Scotland. Trump built a large golf resort in Aberdeenshire and is considered an expert on tourism. On his visit to the Parliament, the US celebrity caused quite an uproar.

Figure 3.5 Donald Trump

Case study: Example of a member's bill

Margo MacDonald MSP – Assisted Suicide Bill

During the current session of parliament (2011 onwards) Margo MacDonald is attempting to introduce a new law that will make assisted suicide legal. Her proposal aims for the introduction of a bill to enable a competent adult with a terminal illness or condition to request assistance to end their own life, and to decriminalise certain actions taken by others to provide such assistance.

The Scottish Parliament will consider the bill during the three-stage process before it potentially becomes law.

What tasks do MSPs complete in the constituency/region?

For MSPs, it is very important that they carry out as many tasks in their constituencies or regions as they can because ultimately it is the people in their constituencies who have the power to keep them in a job at election time.

Conflict between constituency and regional MSPs

Owing to the nature of the electoral system in Scotland, we are represented by both constituency and regional MSPs. Within the eight regions of Scotland there are 73 constituencies, and so areas are represented by both regional MSPs and a constituency MSP. For example, in the 2011 election Derek Mackay (SNP) was elected as the constituency MSP for Renfrewshire North and West.

Show your understanding

1   What is a 'motion'?
2   'Motions are pointless and even if they are debated in Parliament nothing ever happens.' Provide evidence to oppose this statement.
3   Describe, in detail, what happens at General Question Time.
4   Why is asking questions a useful tool at the disposal of MSPs?
5   Describe First Minister's Question Time.
6   Who is currently the First Minister of Scotland?
7   Why do you think opposition MSPs would want to 'catch out' the First Minister?
8   What is the role of a committee in the Scottish Parliament?
9   How many committees are there and on average how many members does each committee have?
10 Look at the Case Study of the Justice Committee.
    (a) When does the committee meet?
    (b) Who is the convener?
    (c) Describe the work the committee undertook in 2012.
11 Look at the Case Study of the Economy, Energy and Tourism Committee.
    (a) When does the committee meet?
    (b) Who is the convener?
    (c) Describe the work the committee undertook in 2012.
12 What is a 'members' bill'?
13 How many members' bills were successful in the last session of Parliament?
14 Describe 'Decision Time' in the Scottish Parliament.

Branch out

15 Look at the examples of questions asked at First Minister's Question Time. Write down three questions you would like to ask the First Minister at his Question Time.

Interview with George Adam MSP

George Adam first got involved with the SNP as a teenager. He was elected as the Member of the Scottish Parliament for Paisley following the 2011 Scottish Parliament Election. He was born and brought up in Paisley and continues to live there. Before his election as an MSP he was a Corporate Sales Manager in the motor industry.

Why did you want to become an MSP?

I had worked as a local councillor in Paisley and decided to stand for Parliament because I wanted to represent this great town and people of Paisley at parliamentary level.

Describe your job

Very busy and exciting. No two days are the same and it is very challenging. My days in my constituency office are made up of meetings with constituents who are looking for advice and help, and meetings with local businesses and community groups. Often they are looking for advice on funding or asking me for support. It is especially a privilege to meet and work with so many fantastic people who are looking to promote Paisley. Working with such groups as the Paisley Development Trust is a real bonus of the job.

What is the most challenging part of your work in Parliament?

The many varied constituency cases and some of the very difficult challenges constituents face. Sometimes not being able to bring a case to a successful conclusion can be heartbreaking for me and my constituency team.

What do you enjoy most about working in the constituency?

Working and representing the good people of Paisley. The interaction with the public is my

Figure 3.6 George Adam

favourite part of the job. You have to enjoy working with people to enjoy this job.

How do you balance the demands of your constituency and party?

I am first and foremost elected to represent the people of Paisley; however, I am very fortunate that my party is very in tune with the Scottish public. Much of the constituency work I do involves matters which aren't party political, so I am able to use my judgement and experience gained from working with so many knowledgeable people, to best advise my constituents.

Do you have much free time as an MSP?

Not really because the minute you cross your doorstep you are working; but I love it. In my free time I go to St Mirren football games and a real plus of this job is getting to work with the club on so many different projects.

However, voters in the Renfrewshire North and West constituency are also represented by seven regional MSPs who cover the West Scotland region. Naturally MSPs come into conflict over duties and issues but this system ensures MSPs work hard to satisfy their constituents.

Attending meetings

MSPs often meet with a wide variety of people in their local constituencies. Councillors, local organisations and local pressure groups all want to meet with MSPs in the hope that any issues they have can be raised at the highest levels of government. Equally, MSPs want to meet these groups in order to stay up to date with issues affecting people in their constituencies. They also want to meet councillors in order to raise issues identified by communicating with constituents through letters, emails, social networking or meetings. They meet these people for discussions regarding a huge variety of issues such as the local environment and planned changes to local areas. A pressure group may want to try to persuade an MSP to raise an issue affecting them in Parliament or even try to get an MSP's public support for their campaign.

Visits and social events

An MSP is regarded as a high-profile guest by many different organisations and so MSPs may spend a large proportion of their time attending various events – for example, the opening of a new business or an awards ceremony. These events are often reported in the local media and provide an opportunity for MSPs to raise their profile in their constituency. MSPs are also keen to visit local schools, especially to meet Modern Studies pupils. Why not contact your MSP and invite him or her to your class?

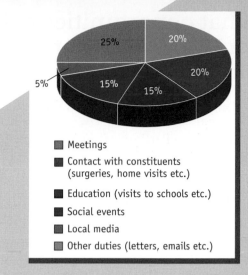

Figure 3.7 An MSP's tasks in the constituency

Local party meetings

MSPs occasionally meet with local party members to discuss issues which concern the party as a whole. This also allows the MSP to meet like-minded individuals and discuss possible new policies or plans for the constituency.

Local media

In order to keep a good profile within their constituency, MSPs often appear in local newspapers or on local TV and radio. This represents an effective way of keeping potential voters aware of work done by MSPs. Quite often MSPs will raise awareness of local issues or highlight local charities using the media and communicate their thoughts about these issues. If an MSP does not use the media effectively it could potentially be damaging for their re-election prospects.

What opportunities exist for constituents to contact MSPs directly?

All MSPs receive a large volume of communication from their constituents. These can take the form of letters sent to Parliament or their constituency office; MSPs constantly receive emails to their official email address; and most MSPs are now in almost daily contact with constituents via social networking sites such as Twitter and Facebook.

MSPs have a small team of staff based at their constituency offices who prioritise letters and emails. Increasingly, MSPs are communicating directly with constituents via social networking. This allows MSPs to keep up to date with events taking place in the constituency and to answer any queries while on the move. A good MSP aims to reply to all communications as swiftly as possible.

Surgeries

An MSP visits different areas of the constituency for an open advice clinic known as a surgery, usually scheduled at a fixed time once a week. Constituents do not need to make an appointment and can drop in to the surgery to express concerns that they have directly to their MSP. These concerns could be about local or national issues. Some MSPs are now holding online surgeries where they can be directly contacted through their personal websites.

Andy Stenhouse @andystenhouseMSP
Constituents – come to my surgery today at Havenside community centre. Here from 1pm to discuss any issues or problems. #helpingwhenican

Andy Stenhouse @andystenhouseMSP
Opening the new local business park today. Great to see new jobs and prosperity coming to Havenside. Come and join the celebrations.

Andy Stenhouse @andystenhouseMSP
@havensidegreenalliance plans for new golf resort in Havenside countryside not yet published. Check local press and council website for details.

Andy Stenhouse @andystenhouseMSP
Fantastic day visiting Havenside Secondary. Modern Studies pupils raised issues over independence, local sports facilities and jobs #futureMSPs. Managed to talk my way into presenting @ pupil's award ceremony.

Show your understanding

1   Look at Figure 3.7. What percentage of time do MSPs spend with their constituents?
2   Explain, in detail, each of the following activities done by MSPs:
    (a) attending meetings
    (b) visits and social events
    (c) going to local party meetings
    (d) appearing in local media.
3   What different forms of communication do MSPs receive from their constituents?
4   Why are MSPs increasingly using social media sites like Twitter and Facebook?
5   Why do you think it is important that an MSP replies swiftly to constituents?
6   Describe an MSP's 'surgery'.

7   Look at the Twitter feed for Andy Stenhouse MSP. From his tweets, describe how he is working with and helping his constituents.

Develop your skills
8   'MSPs spend most of their time at social events when they are in the constituency.' (*Kirsty Gillespie*)
    Using Figure 3.7, explain how Kirsty Gillespie could be accused of exaggeration.

Branch out
9   Think about your own home area. What problems or issues would you like your MSP to act on? Explain why you feel this way.

Added value

Some people argue that politicians should be banned from using social media sites. Investigate the arguments for and against and present your conclusion supporting or opposing the idea of a ban. In doing this, you could create a poster or a PowerPoint presentation.

What challenges exist for MSPs?

The primary job of MSPs is to represent their constituents. However, they have a whole series of different and conflicting pressures to contend with. MSPs are also answerable to the political party they are attached to, and they have to ensure that they have a good relationship with local and national media, and with local and national pressure groups. Added into this mix is trying to ensure a work–life balance in order to spend time with family and friends.

MSPs often find that they cannot keep everyone happy and so they need to manage their decisions carefully, after considering all of these different demands. Occasionally a decision an MSP makes may seem like the wrong one to some and the right decision to others.

Local constituents

MSPs are voted in by their constituents and they have to represent their areas well. If they are judged to have not performed in the interests of their constituents, they might lose their job as people will vote for someone else at the next election.

Political parties

Most MSPs are attached to a political party. This means that they have been selected by local party members to run as a candidate for their political party, and that their campaign will

be funded by the party, who will provide a campaign team to distribute campaign materials and drum up support. This gives candidates a huge advantage.

Part of this agreement is that MSPs, once elected, will attempt to carry out the promises made in the party's manifesto and will support the party when called upon. In addition, candidates know that many voters will vote for a political party regardless of the candidate. Indeed, many voters will not know who their candidates are but will vote for a

Case study: A conflict of loyalties for Havenside MSP

Andy Stenhouse MSP must decide!

Plans for a new multi-million pound world-class golf course in Havenside have been unveiled. It is estimated that the new golf resort will bring over two hundred new jobs to the area as well as bringing in £3 million annually from tourism. This could be a massive boost for Havenside at a time when the economic recession is causing high unemployment among its residents.

Andy Stenhouse MSP must decide whether or not to give his backing to the project. The golf resort is to be built in the countryside, which may conflict with Mr Stenhouse's personal views – he is a committed environmentalist and has always stated that Scotland's countryside should be protected and conserved. The local pressure group Havenside Green Alliance is expecting Mr Stenhouse to shun the golf course.

His party, however, while supporting the conservation of Scotland's countryside, believes that the golf resort has too many benefits to turn it down and should be seriously considered. The party is worried that if the world-class golf resort is rejected many people in the Havenside area may decide to vote for another party at the next election. They expect Andy Stenhouse to back the golf course.

political party to carry out the promises it makes in its manifesto. This means that MSPs recognise that the political party they are attached to has a big influence over their decision making at a local and national level.

Party whips

When MSPs are attending Parliament the political party has a lot of influence on their decision making. It is the party which often dictates how an MSP votes in Parliament. To ensure MSPs carry out the wishes of the party, **party whips** are appointed by the leadership. Whips are men and woman whose job it is to persuade or pressure MSPs to support the party or **follow the party line**. The term 'whips' comes from Westminster and is an informal term to describe people who make sure the party is working together.

 Show your understanding

1. What is an MSP's primary job?
2. What pressures do MSPs have to deal with?
3. Why is representing constituents the most important role for an MSP?
4. Give two reasons why an MSP would want to be a member of a political party.
5. 'MSPs know that the main reason they were elected was because of the party they are attached to.'
   To what extent do you agree with the above statement?
6. Describe the role of the party whip.
7. Read the case study about the conflict of loyalties for Andy Stenhouse.
   (a) What benefits would the golf resort bring to Havenside?
   (b) Why might some people be opposed to the golf course?
   (c) What is Andy's political party's stance on the course?

Branch out

8. In your opinion, should Andy Stenhouse back the golf resort or not? Justify your answer.

 Added value

Research the various ways MSPs can represent their constituents. You could write to your MSP for help and information. You may wish to present your findings in the form of a written piece such as a magazine interview with your local MSP.

Representation of MSPs in the Scottish Parliament

It is desired by all parliaments in the democratic countries of the world that the elected body should be representative of the country's population. That means the percentage of gender and ethnic groups in parliament should reflect the percentage within the population. One of the founding principles of the Scottish Parliament is 'equal opportunity', meaning that people from wide and varied backgrounds should be able to succeed and advance in Scottish society. Politics should be an example of this aim working in practice.

Representation of women

In looking at the composition of the 2011 Scottish parliament we can see that women are not fairly represented in Scottish politics. With 49% of the Scottish population being female there should technically be 63 women MSPs (49% of 129). Unfortunately, the number of female MSPs falls far short of this figure and currently stands at 45. This is a slight improvement from the 2007 election when only 43 women were elected. Table 3.1 shows the figures from 1999 to 2011; during this time the female-to-male ratio of the population remained constant at 49%:51%.

Representation of ethnic minorities

It is an even less positive picture when analysing the representation of ethnic minorities in the 2011 Scottish Parliament. Only two ethnic minority

Election year	Number of male MSPs	As percentage of MSPs	Number of female MSPs	As percentage of MSPs
1999	81	64%	48	36%
2003	78	60.5%	51	39.5%
2007	86	66.6%	43	33.4%
2011	84	65.1%	45	34.9%

Table 3.1 Female/male representation in the Scottish Parliament

Election year	Ethnic population of Scotland	Number of ethnic minority MSPs	As percentage of MSPs
1999	2%	0	0%
2003	2.2%	0	0%
2007	2.7%	1	0.8%
2011	3%	2	1.6%

Table 3.2 Ethnic minority representation in the Scottish Parliament

MSPs were elected in 2011, although this is an improvement on one in 2007. The first two elections in Scottish parliamentary history returned zero ethnic minority MSPs.

Scottish Parliament compared with other parliaments

In terms of fair representation of women, the Scottish Parliament ranks 20th in the world, trailing behind countries like Sweden and Finland, which have over 40% representation. Perhaps surprisingly, the country that has the most women in parliament is Rwanda, with 56.3%. However, they do have a higher female population of around 54%. The UK Parliament ranks 56th in the world with only 22.3% female Members of Parliament (144 out of 650).

The UK Parliament does reflect ethnic minority representation slightly more favourably, with 27 MPs from 650. This is just over 4% of the elected Parliament, against Scotland's 1.6%.

 Show your understanding

1 Equal opportunity was one of the founding principles of the Scottish Parliament. What does this mean?
2 Explain why the representation of women in the current Scottish Parliament (2011–15) is unfair.
3 Look at Table 3.1. How many male and female MSPs were there in 2003?
4 Looking at Table 3.2, how many ethnic minority MSPs were elected in 2011?
5 Why could this be seen as a step forward?
6 How does the Scottish Parliament compare with other countries in terms of female representation?
7 How does the Scottish Parliament compare with the UK Parliament in terms of ethnic minority representation?

Develop your skills

8 'From 1999 until now, the Scottish Parliament has improved the representation of women and ethnic minorities.' *(Hari Singh)*

Using Tables 3.1 and 3.2, explain to what extent Hari Singh could be accused of exaggeration.

Figure 3.8 First Minister Alex Salmond

What are the different roles within the Scottish Parliament?

The debating chamber of the Scottish Parliament is organised in a semicircle. The idea of this layout is to encourage **consensus** among politicians, as opposed to the system used in the House of Commons where parties sit facing each other, which is said to promote **confrontation**.

Who have the most powerful roles in the Scottish parliament?

First Minister

The First Minister is simply the leader of the party that holds power in the Scottish Parliament and is therefore leader of the Scottish government. Currently Alex Salmond of the SNP is Scotland's First Minister. The First Minister has the power to appoint MSPs to become cabinet secretaries and ministers who form the executive (government). He also has the power to 'reshuffle' his cabinet and replace any secretaries whom he feels are underperforming. The First Minister sets the

---

FACT FILE

Who does what in the Scottish Parliament

First Minister: The political leader of Scotland and head of the Scottish government.

Cabinet (secretaries): MSPs from the party in power who have responsibility for a government department.

Junior ministers: MSPs from the party in power who have been given responsibility for assisting a cabinet secretary with a particular department.

Government: Responsible for introducing new legislation and generally managing the devolved affairs of Scotland.

Presiding officer: The Speaker of the Scottish Parliament who controls debates, Question Time and voting.

Opposition parties: Parties who have elected MSPs but are not in power. They are able to hold the government to account in the Parliament.

Opposition leaders: MSPs who are the leaders of the opposition parties. They have extended opportunity to question the government.

Shadow cabinets: MSPs from opposition parties who 'shadow' the work of cabinet secretaries and hold them to account.

Backbench MSPs: MSPs who are not government ministers or shadow government ministers. Most MSPs are backbenchers.

---

agenda and chairs cabinet meetings and is primarily responsible for the formulation and introduction of Scottish government policy. Alex Salmond is in a particularly powerful position concerning the introduction of new laws as his party enjoys a **majority in parliament**, meaning that any bills that pass through will usually receive the necessary number of votes to become law.

The First Minister is also the face of the Scottish government and represents Scotland in devolved matters as well as representing Scotland abroad when building foreign relations.

First Minister	Term of office	Reason for end of office
Donald Dewar	May 1999–October 2000	Died
Henry McLeish	October 2000–November 2001	Resigned
Jack McConnell	November 2001–May 2007	Lost election
Alex Salmond	May 2007–present	

Table 3.6 First Ministers of the Scottish Parliament

The First Minister's powers are kept in check by being held accountable to the Scottish Parliament. The First Minister faces questions every Thursday in First Minister's Question Time, when opposition leaders scrutinise his government's work.

Cabinet

The cabinet is made up of MSPs selected by the First Minister to run specific government departments. Nicola Sturgeon, for example, is Deputy First Minister and Cabinet Secretary for Infrastructure, Investment and Cities. There is a government department for each of the main devolved powers. Running a government department is a promoted post and consequently makes the MSP a senior minister; however, they are referred to as **cabinet secretaries**.

Government

The First Minister selects MSPs to be part of his or her government. These MSPs are usually those who have been most loyal to their party leader. Within the government is the cabinet, who are MSPs in charge of specific government departments. In addition, there are a number of **junior ministers** who help the government ministers run their departments.

Show your understanding

1. What was significant about the result of the 2011 Scottish Parliament election?
2. Why is the Scottish Parliament often referred to as Holyrood?
3. Describe the layout of the debating chamber in the Scottish Parliament.
4. Explain the roles of the following:
   (a) presiding officer
   (b) opposition parties
   (c) backbench MSPs.
5. What are the powers of the First Minister?
6. Why is Alex Salmond in a good position to introduce new laws?
7. How are the First Minister's powers kept in check?
8. Explain, in detail, the roles of the following:
   (a) the cabinet
   (b) the leaders of the opposition.

ICT task

Visit www.scottish.parliament.uk/visitandlearn/Education/12268.aspx. Here you will find interactive resources and games that will help you explore the Parliament building and learn about its functions.

Leaders of the opposition

The leaders of the opposition parties in Scotland do not have any direct power in the Parliament but they are seen as the chief critics of the government. They enjoy a high profile in the media and can have a huge influence over the popularity of a government. They aim to 'score points' over the First Minister in an attempt to show the public that they and their party would be better in power after the next election.

Executive bills

Executive is another word for government, therefore Executive bills are bills introduced by the government. This is done either by a cabinet secretary or by a government minister. The great majority of bills are Executive bills.

The Alcohol (Minimum Pricing) (Scotland) Bill was introduced by Nicola Sturgeon and passed in June 2012. This bill will end cheap alcoholic drink prices in Scotland.

Members' bills

An MSP who is not a member of the government may introduce two bills in each parliamentary session. Around a quarter of new bills are members' bills.

The Control of Dogs (Scotland) Bill was introduced by Christine Grahame and passed in May 2010. This bill allows local authorities to impose measures on people who fail to control a dangerous dog.

Committee bills

Committee bills are initiated by parliamentary committees (see pages 69–70). Only three committee bills have ever become new laws.

Private bills

Private bills can be introduced by a person, group or company and are sometimes known as 'personal bills'. These bills are rarer and are subject to a different scrutiny process.

In 2007, Strathclyde Passenger Transport had a bill passed by the Scottish Parliament that authorised the construction of a railway through a public space.

Public petitions

A petition is a direct way for people to raise a 'national issue' with the Parliament in the hope of changing or introducing a new law. The more signatures a petition gets the better. The petition is then considered by the Public Petitions Committee to decide on what action should be taken. The Smoking Ban in Public Places was first raised as a public petition.

www

Visit www.scottish.parliament.uk/gettinginvolved/petitions/to check out current petitions or even to start one of your own!

How does the Scottish Parliament create new laws?

The Scottish Parliament can make laws on devolved matters. Proposals for any new laws are introduced in parliament as **bills**. There are four different types of bills to ensure that various types of people can attempt to introduce new laws in Scotland. This is important as the Scottish Parliament aims to be open, fair and accessible. The four types of bills are:

- Executive bill
- Member's bill
- Committee bill
- Private bill

How does a bill become a law?

To ensure that laws are created in an open and fair manner a bill has to pass through a **three-stage process** before it becomes a law. This allows the finer details of a bill to be scrutinised, amendments to be made if necessary, and for the Parliament to vote on the bill. If a bill is passed by Parliament it then receives **Royal Assent** (see Figure 3.9).

Royal Assent: When a bill has been passed by the Scottish Parliament, the Queen is asked for her approval. When it has been signed by her, it becomes an Act of the Scottish Parliament.

Stage 1
The appropriate parliamentary committee(s) take evidence on the bill and produce a report on its general principles.

A meeting of the Parliament then considers the report and debates whether to agree to the bill's general principles. Parliament will debate whether the bill should proceed during Decision Time.

If the Parliament agrees, the bill moves on to Stage 2.

If the Parliament does not agree, the bill will fall.

Stage 2
The bill is considered in detail, and scrutinised line by line by a committee or, occasionally, by a committee of the whole Parliament.

Changes to the bill, known as **amendments**, can be made at this stage.

If the Parliament agrees, the bill moves on to Stage 3.

If Parliament does not agree, the bill will fall.

Stage 3
The bill is considered by the whole Parliament.

Amendments to the bill can also be made at this stage. Only amendments made at this stage are debated.

The Parliament then votes on the bill.

If the Parliament agrees, the bill is passed, signed by the monarch and becomes an Act of Parliament.

If Parliament does not agree, the bill will fall.

Figure 3.9 The legislative process in the Scottish Parliament

Case study: A bill becomes law

Offensive Behaviour at Football and Threatening Communications (Scotland) Bill

Type of Bill: Executive

Proposed by: Kenny MacAskill MSP, Justice Minister

Details: The bill creates two new offences – one dealing with offensive behaviour relating to football games, and a second on threatening communications.

Offence 1 deals with sectarian and other offensive chanting and behaviour likely to cause public disorder at football matches.

Offence 2 deals with serious threats – including murder – made on the Internet on sites such as Facebook and Twitter.

Passage of bill: Passed all three stages and received Royal Assent in January 2012.

Show your understanding

1 Create a mind map with 'Various types of bills' in the centre circle. Describe the four types of bill around the outside.

2 Passing a law in the Scottish Parliament involves different stages. Copy and complete the following table to summarise what happens at each stage. Use Figure 3.9 to help you.

Stage	What happens?
Stage 1	
Stage 2	
Stage 3	
Royal Assent	

Achievements of the Scottish Parliament and the impact of devolution

Since its first meeting in 1999, the Scottish Parliament has had four sessions, spanning over a decade. The Parliament has undoubtedly been successful in bringing decision making closer to the people of Scotland, considering that political decisions before 1999 were made in Westminster with the input of English MPs. However, the question many people ask is: has the Scottish Parliament been successful enough?

The Scottish Parliament faced a difficult start with the death of the first First Minister, Donald Dewar, in 2000. The Parliament managed to stabilise and for two sessions (from 1999 to 2007) was led by a Labour–Liberal Democrat coalition. During this time the Parliament had successes, with several high-profile achievements, such as the ban on smoking in public places, which has certainly helped improve Scotland's appalling health record. The Labour–Liberal Democrat coalition also introduced free personal care for the elderly, abolished the Graduate Endowment Tax and banned fox hunting with dogs in 2002.

A new era began in the Scottish Parliament in 2007, when the SNP narrowly beat Labour by one seat and formed a minority government. Since coming to power the SNP have abolished bridge tolls in Scotland, outlawed offensive, sectarian and threatening behaviour at football matches, reintroduced free prescriptions, and introduced minimum pricing for alcohol. A plan to allow gay marriage is also in place.

However, the Scottish Parliament has also had its critics. There was controversy at the construction of the Holyrood building when the budget spiralled out of control and cost the taxpayer over £400 million. Many people also argue that the Parliament could have achieved more for the people of Scotland and that the Parliament needs more powers to be fully effective.

The Scottish government must now manage its budget, not in a period of financial growth as was the situation between 1999 and 2007, but in a period of financial austerity and severe cuts to the budget. In October 2010 Chancellor George Osborne announced that between 2010 and 2015 £81 billion of cuts would be made to reduce the budget deficit. The welfare budget would be cut by £18 million. Scotland has taken its share of these cuts and this means a reduced **block grant** for the Scottish government. Cuts have been made to all services – including education, police and local government – and the cuts to the welfare budget will increase child poverty.

Block grant: The annual amount of money given to Scotland from the UK Treasury.

Show your understanding

1 In your opinion, has the Scottish Parliament been successful? Write a paragraph justifying your answer.

Scotland's future and the independence referendum

We are at a very interesting and exciting time in the history of Scottish politics. The next few years could see historic changes that will affect the Scottish nation and its people forever. In 2014 Scots will have the chance to vote for independence. If they vote 'yes', Scotland will break away from the United Kingdom and become a nation state.

Edinburgh Agreement October 2012

After months of tense negotiations surrounding the independence referendum, the Scottish First Minister, Alex Salmond, and the UK Prime Minister, David Cameron, signed a detailed 30-clause agreement in Edinburgh, agreeing to hold a referendum before the end of 2014.

One of the key elements of the agreement is that the referendum will ask only **one question** as opposed to the two desired by the SNP. The second question the SNP wanted to pose was to ask the electorate whether they wanted more powers for the Scottish Parliament – known as 'devomax'. The SNP successfully negotiated a change to the voting age which means that **16 and 17 year-olds will be allowed to vote** in the referendum – a first for people of this age group in the UK. The signing of the agreement was a historic day for Scotland and a step closer to the possibility of independence.

Case study: Scotland's future: independence and devomax

Before the 2011 election, the SNP promised in their manifesto that, if they won, they would 'put the independence question to the Scottish people'. When the SNP won with a sizeable majority, it gave them a **political mandate** to press forward with the referendum, as the Scottish electorate had backed their promises. ➡

Why an independence referendum?

Within Scotland there has always been some support among the general public for Scotland's return to independence. With the rise of the SNP over the last decade this support has increased. However, many Scots are also against independence and believe Scotland's place should remain within the UK. Many of these people think the solution lies in greater powers for the Scottish Parliament – this is known as **devomax**. Devomax essentially gives the Scottish Parliament maximum powers over all laws, taxes and duties in Scotland, with the exception of defence, foreign affairs and currency.

What question will the independence referendum ask?

When the Scottish people go to the polls in 2014 to decide on Scotland's constitutional future, they will have to answer yes or no to one simple question. The question that will be asked will be worded like this:

Referendum on Scottish independence	
Should Scotland be an independent country?	
Vote (X) in one box only.	
Yes	
No	

September 2012	Results of SNP public consultation published
February 2013	Referendum bill introduced in Scottish Parliament
October 2013	Bill completes all stages and is passed
November 2013	Publication of White Paper on independence
June 2014	Official regulated campaign begins
October 2014	Referendum takes place

Table 3.7 Proposed key dates in the run-up to the independence referendum ➡

What are Scottish political parties doing now in preparation for the referendum?

Campaigning towards the referendum began in 2012. The SNP are obviously campaigning for independence, while Labour, the Conservatives and the Liberal Democrats are all coming together to oppose independence and promote the UK status quo.

SNP Yes Scotland campaign

In May 2012 Alex Salmond launched the SNP's Yes Scotland campaign in a bid to persuade four million Scottish voters that voting for independence would be the right choice. The campaign will run until the referendum in 2014 and has the backing of celebrities, including actors Sir Sean Connery and Brian Cox. The SNP have a special pro-independence declaration – and are urging a million Scots to put their names to it on a new website at www.yesscotland.net. The SNP will also be campaigning and canvassing to convince the people of Scotland to vote 'yes'.

Better Together campaign

In June 2012 Labour, the Conservatives and the Liberal Democrats put their political differences aside to launch the Better Together campaign. The pro-union, anti-independence campaign will aim to convince the Scottish people to vote 'no' to independence in 2014. The campaign will be spearheaded by former UK Chancellor Alistair Darling, with the slogan 'We get the best of both worlds as part of the United Kingdom.' The Better Together campaign will also have the backing of UK politicians including the prime minister. Find out more here: www. bettertogether.net.

Figure 3.10 The Yes Scotland campaign launch

A stronger Scotland, a United Kingdom

Figure 3.11 The Better Together campaign launch

Show your understanding

1   Explain why the SNP have a 'political mandate' to hold an independence referendum.
2   Why is a referendum on independence required?
3   What is 'devomax'?
4   Describe the Yes Scotland campaign.
5   Describe the Better Together campaign.

ICT task

Visit the Yes Scotland and the Better Together websites (www. yesscotland.net and www. bettertogether.net). Research the progress of each campaign and what they are doing to convince the Scottish public to support them.

Local government in Scotland

How is local government in Scotland organised?

Local government is often overshadowed by the magnitude of national politics in Scotland. However, local government is massively important as it is the first stage of representation for people in Scotland. It also plays a significant and essential role in people's everyday lives. For example, it is local councils who run our schools and decide if your school should get funding for extra computers or for new windows or maintenance. It is local councils who take charge of refuse collection and who pick up our recycling on a weekly basis. Further to this, local councils are in charge of services like social work, roads and transport, housing, libraries, and leisure services such as football pitches, parks and swimming pools. These are only a few of the many areas that local councils are tasked to organise, fund and manage – so, as you can imagine, local councils have a lot of responsibility.

Because of the responsibility of managing many important services, local councils require elected representatives to serve as **councillors**. Depending on the population of the council

What you will learn:

1 How local government is organised.
2 The various services local councils provide.
3 The work undertaken by councillors and the challenges they face.

area, a certain number of councillors are elected by the voters. Councillors represent a political party and the party with the majority of elected councillors is the 'ruling group'. It is these elected councillors who make decisions that affect our local services. Following the 2012 Scottish local council elections, Glasgow City Council is run by the Labour group. This is because Labour managed to secure 44 of the 79 available seats.

The services that local councils provide are either **mandatory** or **discretionary** (see Table 3.8). Mandatory services are services that councils are required to provide by law, whereas discretionary services are provided by the council's own choice.

Discretionary services can sometimes be controversial, as offering these services eats into the council's budget. For example, every year Renfrewshire Council organises a Christmas concert, and in 2011 paid £15,000 to pop star Stacey Solomon to switch on the Christmas lights.

The structure of local government

Before 1996 local government in Scotland was rather complicated, as it was based on a two-tier system. Scotland was divided into nine large 'regional councils', each containing numerous smaller 'district councils' that represented a smaller area. One of these regions was called Strathclyde Regional Council and included 19 different district councils.

Local government is now a simple single-tier system with Scotland divided into 32 councils (local authorities) stretching from Shetland

Mandatory services	Discretionary services
Education	Leisure facilities
Social work	Parks and recreation
Housing	Community centres
Environmental services	Gala days

Table 3.8 Mandatory and discretionary service provided by local councils

	Population	Area (sq km)
Scotland	5,222,100	77,925
Aberdeen City	217,120	186
Aberdeenshire	245,780	6,313
Angus	110,570	2,182
Argyll & Bute	89,200	6,909
Clackmannanshire	50,630	159
Dumfries & Galloway	148,190	6,426
Dundee City	144,290	60
East Ayrshire	120,240	1,262
East Dunbartonshire	104,580	175
East Lothian	97,500	679
East Renfrewshire	89,540	174
Edinburgh, City of	486,120	264
Eilean Siar (Western Isles)	26,190	3,071
Falkirk	153,280	297
Fife	365,020	1,325
Glasgow City	592,820	175
Highland	221,630	25,659
Inverclyde	79,770	160
Midlothian	81,140	354
Moray	87,720	2,238
North Ayrshire	135,180	885
North Lanarkshire	326,360	470
Orkney Islands	20,110	990
Perth & Kinross	147,780	5,286
Renfrewshire	170,250	261
Scottish Borders	112,870	4,732
Shetland Islands	22,400	1,466
South Ayrshire	111,440	1,222
South Lanarkshire	311,880	1,772
Stirling	89,850	2,187
West Dunbartonshire	90,570	159
West Lothian	172,080	427

Table 3.9 Local authorities in Scotland: population and area, 2011

Source: General Register Office for Scotland

in the north to the Scottish Borders in the south. It is claimed that this system allows local government to operate in a more efficient and effective way but critics argue that some councils, such as Clackmannanshire, are too small for this to be the case.

Table 3.9 shows Scotland's 32 local councils. Looking at the table and the map, Highland Council is by far the largest authority in terms of area. However, Glasgow and Edinburgh are by far the largest in terms of population.

What services do local councils provide?

Scottish local government provides many of society's most valued services. These services help children grow and learn, protect and care for the vulnerable, and provide the essential day-to-day services that allow people to work and live in our communities. All 32 local councils provide similar services, but they have to be organised, structured and managed in a way that meets the needs of their local population. For example, the housing department at Glasgow City Council has very different service requirements from those of the housing department at Highland Council. Both have the responsibility of dealing with the homeless but Glasgow has to dedicate a far greater amount of focus and resources on this remit than Highland Council does.

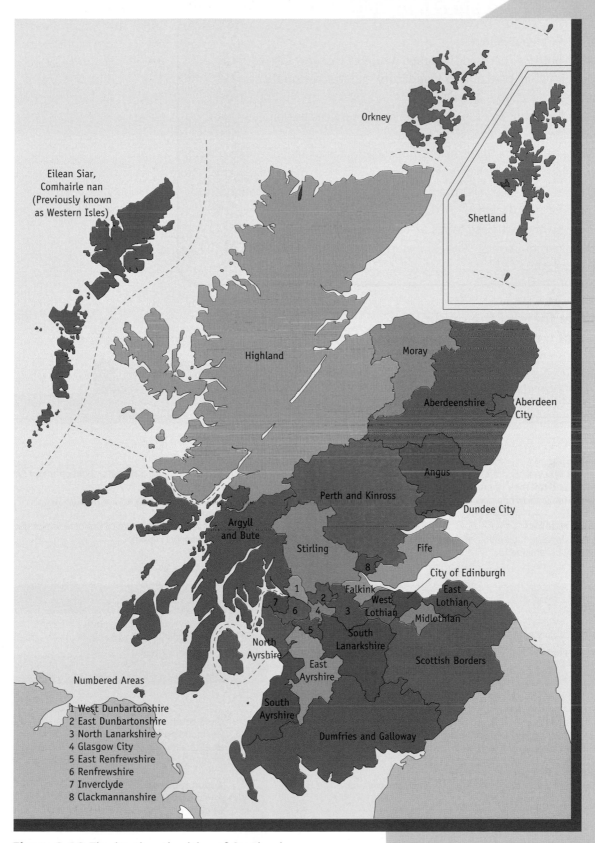

Figure 3.12 The local authorities of Scotland

Orkney

Eilean Siar,
Comhairle nan
(Previously known
as Western Isles)

Shetland

Highland

Moray

Aberdeenshire

Aberdeen
City

Angus

Perth and Kinross

Dundee City

Argyll
and Bute

Stirling

Fife

8

City of Edinburgh

1

Falkink

East
Lothian

7

2

West
Lothian

6

4

3

Midlothian

5

South
Lanarkshire

North
Ayrshire

Scottish Borders

East
Ayrshire

South
Ayrshire

Numbered Areas

Dumfries and Galloway

1 West Dunbartonshire
2 East Dunbartonshire
3 North Lanarkshire
4 Glasgow City
5 East Renfrewshire
6 Renfrewshire
7 Inverclyde
8 Clackmannanshire

Show your understanding

1 What is a councillor?
2 What political party is the ruling group of Glasgow City Council?
3 Explain what is meant by **mandatory** and **discretionary** services, giving an example of each.
4 In pairs, think of as many discretionary services as you can that your local council provides each year.
5 'Since 1996 local government in Scotland has changed.' Give evidence to support this statement.
6 Look at Table 3.9. List the five largest and five smallest councils in terms of population.
7 Refer to the five case briefs below. How do members of the public make use of council services and describe the help provided by the council.

How do members of the public make use of council services on a daily basis?

Department: Housing
Name: Jennifer McMillan
Age: 27

Case brief:
Jennifer is currently homeless. She split up with her partner and left their home in fear of her safety. She has applied for emergency accommodation.

Action required:
Assess Jennifer's situation and advise her on any benefits she may be entitled to.

Department: Environmental Services
Name: Amal Sharma
Age: 42

Case brief:
Amal recently had lunch at a local cafe and later fell ill with food poisoning.

Action required:
An immediate inspection of the cafe is planned by Environmental Health.

Department: Social Work
Name: Annie Lochrie
Age: 80

Case brief:
Annie has applied to the council for Community Care as she requires additional help and support at home.

Action required:
Arrange for a social worker to visit Annie to carry out a home care assessment.

Department: Planning
Name: Raymond Costello
Age: 37

Case brief:
Raymond has applied to obtain planning permission for an extension to his house. This extension may block the amount of natural sunlight his neighbour's garden receives.

Action required:
A Planning Officer will visit Mr Costello and recommend whether or not to grant the application.

Department: Roads and Transport

Name: John Glancy

Age: 49

Case brief:
John contacted the department to inform us of a large pothole on one of our roads that damaged his tyre.

Action required:
The Road Maintenance Team will fill in the pothole as a matter of urgency.

Case study: Stirling Council

Stirling Council lies at the heart of Scotland and serves an area with a population of 89,000. This population is split evenly between urban and rural areas. The urban population mainly centres around the city of Stirling, Dunblane and Bridge of Allan.

Figure 3.13 The logo of Stirling Council

Education and learning

Stirling Council operates 30 nurseries, 40 primary schools and 7 secondary schools. It also makes specialist educational provision such as educational psychologists.

Housing

Affordable rented council housing is available across the council area. The council has to maintain and improve their housing stock and provide tenants with benefits advice. The housing department also works to eradicate homelessness.

Roads and transport

Stirling Council looks after over a thousand miles of road network and has the responsibility of making sure this network is adequately maintained and safe. Along with the roads, the council provides street lighting, traffic signage, traffic calming measures and co-ordinates all roadworks. The council also manages the gritting and snow-clearing service during the winter.

Environmental services

The council has a responsibility to keep the area clean and tidy. This job involves collecting refuse and recycling, street sweeping and maintaining parks and open spaces. Further to this, the council deals with environmental health issues and aims to promote low-carbon sustainable living.

Tourism

Stirling is fortunate to have several historic visitor attractions and the area attracts thousands of visitors each year. The tourism department works to boost tourism through promotion, advertising, and organising events and festivals to bring people to the area.

Law and licensing

This department deals with various areas from birth, death and marriage registrations to licensing and permits for new shops and bars. It also operates the Sheriff and Justice of the Peace courts.

Figure 3.14 This statue of Robert the Bruce is one of the historic visitor attractions in the area.

Leisure services

It is important that the council offers a variety of leisure services. Therefore not only does this department manage recreational services such as leisure centres, swimming pools and gyms, it also manages cultural services such as libraries, museums and art galleries.

Planning

The planning department makes decisions about future developments and the use of land in the towns, cities and countryside of the Stirlingshire area. For example, before the building of a new golf course or supermarket, permission must be gained through this department.

Finance

All revenue received by the council through council tax, government grants, housing rent and so on is managed by the finance department. The department also has the responsibility of ensuring the council is operating financially within budget.

 Show your understanding

1 Which council department in Stirling Council is responsible for each of the following?
   (a) Helping the homeless
   (b) Tourist event at Stirling Castle
   (c) Repairing potholes in the roads
   (d) The Sheriff Court
   (e) Payment of council tax
   (f) Emptying waste bins
   (g) Granting permission for a new cinema
   (h) The registration of a newborn baby
2 Pick three council services and describe how these services meet the needs of people in the local community.

ICT task

Visit the website of your local council and research the various services that the council offers. Create an information leaflet that will inform members of the public about at least *five services* that your council offers. Include a heading with your council's logo beside it, and pictures and graphics to enhance your leaflet.

How is local government financed?

Local councils provide a vast range of services and employ thousands of people. If you think about the total cost of running our schools and all the other services as well as the salaries of all the council staff, it adds up to a staggering amount well into the millions. It may appear that many local council services come 'free of charge'. For example, your parents may not directly pay for you to attend school and we do not directly pay for our refuse to be collected. However, all these services do have to be paid for and the finance to fund local government comes from ordinary people in several ways.

Central government funding

Local councils receive by far the largest part (80%) of their funding from the Scottish government through a grant called Aggregate External Finance. When the Scottish government receives its funding from the UK government, a decision is made about the budget that each local council will be allocated. The 32 local councils do not receive an equal share. The funding that councils receive depends on various factors such as population and social deprivation. With a population of over half a million, Glasgow City Council receives a far greater share than Stirling Council with its population of 89,000. In 2012 the Scottish government provided a funding package to local councils worth £11.5 billion in total. This money comes from various taxes that the government collects from people such as Income Tax and Value Added Tax (VAT).

Council Tax

Another means of income for local government is Council Tax. Each council in Scotland charges an annual tax on property in their area. The amount of Council Tax paid by a house owner depends on the value of the house in which they live. For example, a person living in a small flat will pay less than a family living in a large five-bedroom house. The council bases their tax on two adults living in a property, but gives a 25% reduction if there is only one adult occupier. This has obvious benefits for single parents.

Council Tax is based on property 'valuation bands' that range from A to H. Band A is used for cheaper properties and requires the occupier to pay less Council Tax, and band H is for the most expensive property, requiring the highest Council Tax payment. These values were set in 1991.

On top of the Council Tax charge, local councils also collect an annual payment for sewerage and water, and again these charges are based on the value of the property. Council Tax is the most obvious way that people pay for the services that councils provide, but it makes up only around 12% of the overall funding that councils receive.

Facility service charges

Local councils also receive income through charging people to use their facilities and services. Rental from council housing is the biggest source of income but money is also made from charging people to use swimming pools, gyms, football pitches and so on.

Spending the money

Councils have to use their income to devise a budget that ensures they are spending the public's money wisely and efficiently. You can see from Figure 3.15 that, on average, education takes up almost a third of local council budgets.

Public–private partnerships

Public–private partnerships (PPPs) are joint working contracts made between the public sector (local councils) and the private sector (local businesses). The up-front cost of building new state-of-the-art schools or hospitals is often too expensive for many

Band	Property value	Annual Council Tax
A	below £27,000	£779.33
B	£27,001 to £35,000	£909.22
C	£35,001 to £45,000	£1,039.11
D	£45,001 to £58,000	£1,169.00
E	£58,001 to £80,000	£1,428.78
F	£80,001 to £106,000	£1,688.56
G	£106,001 to £212,000	£1,948.33
H	above £212,000	£2,338.00

Table 3.10 Council Tax valuation bands, Edinburgh City Council, 2012–13

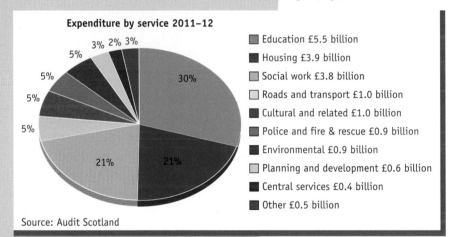

Expenditure by service 2011–12

- Education £5.5 billion
- Housing £3.9 billion
- Social work £3.8 billion
- Roads and transport £1.0 billion
- Cultural and related £1.0 billion
- Police and fire & rescue £0.9 billion
- Environmental £0.9 billion
- Planning and development £0.6 billion
- Central services £0.4 billion
- Other £0.5 billion

Source: Audit Scotland

Figure 3.15 Expenditure in Scottish local authorities, 2011–12

Show your understanding

1 Why is it wrong to describe council services as 'free of charge'?
2 What percentage of local government funding comes from central government?
3 What was the total funding package for local councils in Scotland in 2012?
4 Describe why some people pay more Council Tax than others.
5 What services can councils charge local people to use? Can you give your own examples?
6 Look at Figure 3.15. Which service receives the most money and can you suggest a reason for this?
7 What is a public–private partnership (PPP)?
8 Provide one argument for and one argument against the use of PPPs by local councils.

councils to afford, especially if more than one is required to be built at a time. A way of funding such building projects is through PPP schemes where a local council will allow a private company to build a school or hospital and will then pay the firm back over a period of time. In 2008 Renfrewshire Council saw the completion of ten new schools, including six primary and four secondary schools, two community nurseries and a community learning centre. The council will pay a bill of £135 million over the next 30 years.

The use of PPPs by local councils has been controversial. The obvious benefits include the provision of first-class facilities that a council would not be able to afford to pay for up front. However, many have criticised PPPs, claiming that private companies have made massive profits at the taxpayer's expense.

The work of a local councillor

Each local council is divided into smaller areas called **wards**. Each ward will be represented by around three or four councillors. For example, Dundee City Council has 29 councillors who represent 8 wards.

The job of a councillor centres on working to improve the lives of local people. To help individual residents they hold regular 'surgeries' (as MSPs and MPs do) where local people can bring any problems or concerns they have. The local councillor will work to assist the person in trying to solve their problem or issue.

Councillors are also members of council committees. There is usually a committee for each of the various council departments. A councillor will usually be a member of several, ranging from the Education Committee to the Licensing Committee. As members of such committees, councillors may need to make key decisions that seriously affect their local area.

As well as meetings, councillors have to attend local events such as gala days or the opening of a new school or shopping centre. It is very important that local councillors interact with local people and associate themselves with positive developments in their council area.

Is being a local councillor a 'career'?

Working as a councillor isn't generally regarded as being a career or a profession. This is mainly due to the fact that after four or five years a local councillor could lose his or her seat at the election and so lose the job. Because of this, while in office a local councillor can have another full-time job and fit council duties around that career. However, being a councillor is a very time-consuming and demanding job, so councillors now get a salary of around £16,000 per year plus expenses. There is continued debate over whether councillors should be full-time professionals.

Figure 3.16 Councillor Gordon Matheson opened the new Emirates Arena in Glasgow.

New play park for city scheme

Local residents of a Glasgow housing scheme have been rewarded for their hard work and endeavour after approaching their local councillor about the lack of facilities for young people in their area. The local councillor managed to secure funding from the council to build a play park in their neighbourhood which has in turn reduced antisocial behaviour and crime. Councillor John Herd was very helpful and the people of his ward have heaped praise on him. Resident Jean Mackie said, 'We approached Councillor Herd at his surgery and he was happy to help improve our area.' Without going through the local councillor, the residents might have found it difficult to approach the council themselves, leaving them with no avenues to take their plans forward.

Local primary school set to be closed and bulldozed

Local councillors have taken the decision to close one of Fairburgh Town's oldest primary schools. The popular school is set to be closed and demolished and the land used to build 50 new homes. Councillors from the council's Education Committee blamed high running costs and dwindling pupil numbers for their decision to close Fairburgh Primary School. They said it was operating at 36% capacity, compared with an average of 72% occupancy for other primary schools in the area. Parents and pupils are outraged and upset that their studies will be disrupted to move to another school. One parent remarked, 'This is simply not good enough; schools should not be closing as it causes chaos to the children's education.'

DIARY: COUNCILLOR JOHN HERD (SNP)

Monday	4.00p.m. Deliver leaflets to a residential area in my ward. Aim to talk with locals. 5.00p.m. Surgery in local community centre.
Tuesday	3.00p.m. Education Committee meeting. Agenda includes: budgets for local schools and possible Public Private Partnership scheme to build new secondary schools. 7.30p.m. Attend local secondary school talent show.
Wednesday	4.30p.m. Housing Committee meeting. Agenda includes: redevelopment of tenement flats and building of new housing estate. 6.00p.m. Meeting with local residents to discuss antisocial behaviour issues.
Friday	1.00p.m. Open new business centre on the High Street. 4.00p.m. Full council meeting. 7.00p.m. Attend local charity dinner at the Town Hall with MSP and MP.

Should councillors be full-time?

YES

Councillors could focus solely on council business and devote more time to their constituents.

Councillors would be willing to stay working as a councillor for longer.

A wider variety of people could become councillors as many councillors are retired people with a lot of free time.

NO

The cost of increasing salaries for full-time councillors would be a massive burden on taxpayers' money.

Being a councillor is about helping local people and the community – not about a full-time career!

Some councillors work harder than others … for some it is not a full-time job.

Show your understanding

1 What is the name given to the areas that a council is divided into?
2 Why do councillors hold surgeries?
3 What is a council committee?
4 Look at the newspaper article about the primary school closure.
   (a) Why did councillors have to close Fairburgh Primary School?
   (b) Do you agree with the closure? Justify your answer.
5 Study the diary of Councillor John Herd.
   (a) What two committees is John Herd a member of?
   (b) Why do you think it is important for John Herd to attend a school talent show and a local charity dinner?
6 Why is being a councillor generally not thought of as a profession or a career?
7 What is the annual salary of a councillor?
8 You have learned about the debate surrounding the issue of councillors working full-time. What is your opinion on the debate? Use the diary extract and viewpoints on page 98 to help you justify your answer.

Branch out

9 Write a newspaper article describing a story about a local councillor who has assisted people in his or her ward. It could be about solving conflict, such as a resident who is having problems with noisy neighbours, or it could be about assisting residents with a particular issue, such as the opening of a local community centre.

What challenges exist for local councillors?

Local councillors have to meet the demands and needs of the people they represent. This could mean tackling an issue relating to a housing problem, or protecting a local bus route or even working to regenerate the town centre. In undertaking such tasks, a councillor will come across challenges in the form of conflict – possibly with constituents, other councillors, private companies or even MSPs or MPs. A councillor must be able to mediate and negotiate to find the best possible solution for his or her constituents.

Furthermore, councillors are facing tough **financial challenges**. From 2010 to 2015, the

→ Added value

Being a councillor is a demanding job. Research the positives and negatives of making the job of councillor a full-time position. Create a report for the Scottish government that outlines your arguments and recommendations.

Case study: Scottish council budget cuts

All 32 local councils in Scotland are having to deal with severe budget cuts. Councils have worked out how much needs to be saved by 2015.

Argyll and Bute	£18 million
Aberdeenshire	£62 million
East Dunbartonshire	£15 million
Glasgow City	£127 million
North Lanarkshire	£70 million

Table 3.11 Cuts in selected local councils

revenue grants from the Scottish government are falling from £8.7 billion to £7.9 billion. As a consequence councils are having to make millions of pounds of savings.

How do councils manage budget cuts?

In making savings to their budgets, councils first have to cut jobs. For example, East Dunbartonshire plans to cut the number of staff working in the council by 200 posts per year. These job cuts affect employment levels in the local area.

Councils then have to make big savings on cutting services and increasing charges. This is very unpopular with local people and is therefore difficult for a council to do. Councillors will analyse services and cut the ones that will have less of an impact. For example, Glasgow City Council decided to shut some local libraries. Councils may also look to shut or merge schools where possible, reduce street sweeping, dim non-essential street lighting and charge more for services such as swimming pools or gym membership. Discretionary services such as gala days and festivals may also become victims of cuts.

Show your understanding

1. Who might a councillor come into conflict with when tackling a problem on behalf of a constituent?
2. How much does the Scottish government plan to cut its revenue grants by between 2010 and 2015?
3. Look at Table 3.11.
   (a) Which council is making the biggest cuts?
   (b) Can you think of a reason why Glasgow's cuts are far higher than East Dunbartonshire's?
4. Why is cutting services unpopular with local people?
5. Give examples of ways local councils may try to save money.

Case study: Aberdeen City Council dispute over City Garden project

Figure 3.17 An artist's impression of the Aberdeen City Garden project

In March 2012 almost 100,000 Aberdeen residents voted in a public referendum to support or reject a £140 million plan to regenerate Aberdeen city centre. Fifty-two per cent of voters voted to support the 'City Garden' project that aimed to transform old sunken city gardens into a futuristic new civic square. The plan was then backed by the Liberal Democrat-led council, with a local businessman, Sir Ian Wood, pledging £50 million of his own money to help fund the redevelopment.

However, after the Scottish local council elections in May 2012, Labour (in coalition with the Conservatives) became the leading party in Aberdeen City Council. The new coalition council decided to reject the project and it was scrapped in August 2012.

This was a hugely controversial move by the council because, through the public referendum, the majority of people in Aberdeen had voted 'yes' for the new development. Many business leaders were furious and Sir Ian Wood withdrew his offer of a £50 million assistance fund. Labour council leader Barney Crockett stated, 'the city centre can be regenerated through other means without the massive cost to the taxpayer and the council. The project divided the whole city. Fifty-two per cent was not a firm enough endorsement to press ahead.'

Decision making in local councils

From time to time local councils have to make large-scale decisions that will impact on a whole town or city. Councillors will come together in their political parties to discuss, debate and vote on certain issues, initiatives or projects. Sometimes there will be conflict between political parties who have different views on what will benefit the local area. Ultimately, the ruling party in the council usually has the majority vote on whether to accept or reject new plans or developments.

Political parties in Scotland

What is a political party?

In Scotland there are four main political parties. Three of these parties mirror the three main parties active across the UK: Labour, Conservative and Liberal Democrat. The fourth party is the Scottish National Party (SNP). There are numerous smaller parties active in Scotland, such as the Green Party and the Scottish Socialist Party.

A political party is an organisation made up of people who share similar political beliefs and opinions. A political party ultimately aims to get elected by winning as many seats as possible in Parliament. The more seats that a political party wins, the more influence it can exert over the running of the country. There are 129 available seats for the Scottish Parliament. In 2011, the SNP won 69 of the seats, creating the first **majority government** in Scottish parliamentary history. Therefore the SNP currently holds political power in Scotland. The leader of the party that holds political power is called the **First Minister**.

Political parties continuously try to win support among the general public so that when an election comes round they have a good chance of achieving votes. This can be very expensive and this is one reason why most MSPs are members of a political party rather than independents.

It is very important to political parties that they have a positive public image and a likeable party

Show your understanding

1 Why is there sometimes conflict when a council has to make large-scale decisions?
2 Read the case study on the Aberdeen City Garden project.
   (a) What did the project aim to do?
   (b) Why, after May 2012, was the project rejected?
   (c) Why was the rejection controversial?
   (d) What did council leader Barney Crockett say to justify his party's decision?

What you will learn:

1 What political parties are.
2 The difference between political parties.
3 Who the main political parties in Scotland are.
4 How people participate in Scottish politics.

leader. If the public do not like a party leader, support for the party will drop. In 2011 the Scottish Labour Party suffered a heavy defeat at the hands of the SNP. Many people attributed this loss to the party leader, Iain Gray, whose public image was less than favourable.

Political party	Constituencies/ regions (seats)
SNP	69
Labour	37
Conservative	15
Liberal Democrat	5
Green	2
Independent	1
Total	**129**

Table 3.12 Scottish Parliament election results 2011

What are the differences between the political parties?

Political parties have their own visions and plans for how they think the country should be run. These plans can be listed under key **policy** areas such as education, environment, justice, economy and health. Before an election, each political party publishes a document outlining its policies, known as a **party manifesto**. Each party's manifesto is unique, and one party's visions and plans can differ quite remarkably from another's. The Fact File on each political party tells you a little about each party and some of the policies it believes will make Scotland a better country.

FACTFILE

The Scottish National Party

About

The SNP's popularity in Scotland has increased considerably in the last decade. In Alex Salmond it has a leader who has guided the party to its most successful spell in its history. The party has campaigned for Scottish independence for seven decades and is currently running the 'Yes' campaign in preparation for the 2014 independence referendum. The SNP holds power in Scotland and it also holds six seats in Westminster. Generally speaking, the SNP is supported by all factions and classes of Scottish society. However, as the SNP prepares for the referendum, party leaders are reviewing their policy towards NATO, the military alliance of USA and European countries. (See newspaper article below.)

Key policies

- Continue to campaign for Scottish independence.
- Will not introduce tuition fees or top-up fees for colleges or universities.
- Make Scotland a world leader in green energy.
- Introduce a minimum pricing for alcohol.
- No more nuclear – oppose nuclear weapons.

Figure 3.19 Alex Salmond

www.snp.org

Figure 3.18 The SNP logo

TWO MSPs resign from SNP over party's NATO stance

Two SNP party members of the Scottish Parliament who led a rebellion against proposals for an independent Scotland to join NATO have resigned in protest.

John Finnie and Jean Urquhart announced they had quit after the party very narrowly voted to overturn the decades-long ban on NATO membership at the 2012 Party Conference. John Finnie said: 'I cannot belong to a party that quite rightly does not wish to hold nuclear weapons on its soil [the UK Trident nuclear weapons system is based on the Clyde] but wants to join a first-strike nuclear alliance. I cannot in good conscience continue to take the party whip'.

Adapted from the *Guardian*, 23 October 2012

FACT FILE

The Labour Party

About

The Labour Party, known in Scotland as Scottish Labour, is led by Johann Lamont. Labour has traditionally been a popular party in Scotland with strong support, especially among the working class. However, in 2007 Labour lost control of the Scottish Parliament, and the party performed even worse in the 2011 Scottish election, winning only 37 seats. The party has strong links to trade unions, who influence many of their policies.

Scottish🌹Labour

Figure 3.20 The Scottish Labour Party logo

Key policies

- Keep Scotland part of the UK.
- Scottish Labour would introduce fees of some sort for university students, arguing that places are lost to paying foreign students.
- Prioritise the creation of green jobs, aiming for up to 60,000 by 2015.
- Protect NHS jobs, with no compulsory redundancies for NHS staff.
- Offer a modern apprenticeship to every 16–18-year-old who wants one from 2013.

Figure 3.21 Johann Lamont

FACT FILE

The Conservative Party

About

The Scottish Conservatives are led by Ruth Davidson and the UK party is led by Prime Minister David Cameron. In the 2010 UK election the Conservatives managed to win enough seats to enter a coalition with the Liberal Democrats. However, in Scotland the Scottish Conservatives have not been so successful and they only won 15 seats in the 2011 Scottish Parliament election. The Conservatives struggle in Scotland and have limited support among the Scottish people. This is mainly because of the unpopular Conservative government of the 1980s led by Margaret Thatcher. The support the Conservatives do have in Scotland generally comes from the middle and upper classes.

Figure 3.22 The Scottish Conservative Party logo

Key policies

- Keep Scotland as part of the UK.
- Give head teachers more power over discipline policy, staff recruitment and budgets.
- Introduce tougher jail sentences and end automatic early release from prison.
- Introduce free, universal health checks for those aged between 40 and 74.
- End Scottish government policy against nuclear power – consider new stations.

Figure 3.23 Ruth Davidson

FACT FILE

The Liberal Democrats

About

The Scottish Liberal Democrats are one of the three state parties within the federal Liberal Democrats; the others being the Welsh Liberal Democrats and the Liberal Democrats in England. The Scottish Liberal Democrats hold 5 of 129 seats in the Scottish Parliament, 11 of 59 Scottish seats in the UK Parliament, and one of six Scottish seats in the European Parliament. They are led by Willie Rennie MSP who shot to prominence in the Dunfermline and West Fife by-election in 2006, taking the seat from Labour with a swing of 16%.

Key policies

- Want Scotland to be part of a federal UK. Have outlined plans for more powers for the Scottish Parliament including significant control over tax levers.

- Keep education free, with no tuition fees and no graduate contribution. Protect college funding.

- Support early intervention work, especially in education where they want free childcare for 40% of two-year-olds which would help children from the most deprived backgrounds get the best start in life.

- Support sustainable transport and focus on getting faster and cheaper trains to all parts of Scotland, not just the central belt.

- The only party to oppose the centralisation of Scotland's police and fire services.

Figure 3.24 The Scottish Liberal Democrat Party logo

Figure 3.25 Willie Rennie

Show your understanding

1 Name the four main political parties in Scotland.
2 What is a political party?
3 Which party is in power in Scotland?
4 Why is it important that a party has a likeable leader?
5 What is a party manifesto?
6 Study the Fact File of each political party.
   (a) Who are the leaders of the four parties in Scotland?
   (b) Do any parties have similar policies? If so, name them.
   (c) How many seats did each party win in the 2011 Scottish election?

Branch out

7 Look at the policies of each political party. If you were able to vote, which party would you vote for? Justify your decision by referring to at least two policies.

Participation in Scottish politics

Voting in an election isn't the only way people can take part in politics in Scotland. People who support a political party can get actively involved with that party by joining as a **party member**. How you can become a member of a political party and stand as a candidate in an election is discussed on page 63.

Figure 3.26 Personal qualities of a political candidate

ICT task

Using the Internet, research the policies of a particular Scottish political party of your choice. In groups create a **party political broadcast** (see Chapter 4, page 12) to present to the class at a later date.

Show your understanding

1. What influence does a person have in a political party when they join as a member?
2. Describe the various methods of campaigning that a party member can be involved in at election time.
3. How do you become a political party's candidate for election? (Look back to page 63 to remind yourself.)
4. Study the various personal qualities required to stand as a candidate for a political party. Pick three that you feel are the most important. Explain your choice.

Branch out

5. In pairs, select at least five personal qualities and create a job advertisement or leaflet for Jobcentre Plus. Your advertisement should explain why a candidate and an MSP would need each of the five personal qualities.

Chapter 4

Pressure groups, trade unions and media

Pressure groups

What is a pressure group?

A pressure group is an organisation made up of like-minded individuals who want to influence decision making. Many people have passions in life – perhaps for the environment and living a low-carbon life, or for their local community. In the UK's representative democracy these individuals are constituents and have the right to ask their MP, MSP or councillor to consider their opinion when making decisions. However, these representatives have many different factors to take into account when making decisions and they might not follow the wishes of the constituent. Some individuals feel that they will have more success in pressuring the government as a group rather than as individuals. There are thousands of pressure groups in the UK and they vary in size from a small group of locals protesting about the building of a new supermarket up to multinational organisations protesting about global warming. Pressure groups do not want to be in government or in mainstream politics, as they have an interest only in one particular issue.

What you will learn:

1 What a pressure group is.
2 What the aims of pressure groups are.
3 The methods used by pressure groups.
4 Examples of pressure group action.
5 Issues with pressure groups.

What are the aims of pressure groups?

Every pressure group will have different set of aims. A pressure group may have only one aim. For example the Campaign for Nuclear Disarmament (CND) wants nuclear weapons to be scrapped completely by all nations. It will continue to campaign until this happens. On the other hand, some groups have many aims and many campaigns, such as the Woodhill Residents' Group, which is a small pressure group in the Bishopbriggs area of East Dunbartonshire that campaigns on a number of issues in the area, including banning phone masts, town centre regeneration and reducing speed limits. The aims of pressure groups can be classified by what type of pressure group they are (see Table 4.1).

Examples of pressure groups

Amnesty International – a multinational group which campaigns for human rights.

BMA – the British Medical Association represents the interests of doctors.

CBI – the Confederation of British Industry promotes the wishes of UK businesses.

Greenpeace – campaigns on a global scale on environmental issues.

Mumsnet – represents the views of parents and influences decision makers in their policy making (see page 110).

Scottish SPCA – campaigns for more laws preventing cruelty to animals.

Sustainable Aberdeenshire – a temporary pressure group set up in protest at Donald Trump's Menie Estate golf course. It has since disbanded.

Cause groups	Sectional groups
Members who join these groups have concerns about a specific issue.	Members join these groups because they represent their position in employment or society.
These groups are open to nearly everybody and number in their thousands.	These groups are exclusive to their members and are closed to many. The most well-known of these groups are trade unions.
Some groups are small and may be only temporary, depending on the issue at stake.	Groups will be well organised.
Others may be decades old and campaign on a global scale.	They will campaign on many issues which affect their members.
Many of these pressure groups are also registered charities.	They are often more successful than cause groups as they can threaten industrial action.

Table 4.1 Types of pressure groups

 Show your understanding

1 What is a pressure group?
2 Why do some people feel the need to form a pressure group?
3 Explain three key differences between cause groups and sectional groups.
4 Look at the list of examples of pressure groups. Draw up a list with two headings – Cause Group and Sectional Group – and decide which heading each should be put under.

ICT task

Working in pairs, use the Internet to research a pressure group of your choice. Prepare a 3–5 slide presentation to report back to your class or group. You may want to find out the following information:

• How and when was it established?
• What are its core aims?
• How many members does it have?
• Two examples of action that it has taken.

 Added value

You could create a wiki about a pressure group of your choice. Your wiki could provide background information about the group and an analysis of how effective the group's methods have been.

What methods do pressure groups use?

In a democratic society, members of the public are allowed to express their views and have the right to disagree publicly with decision makers. As a result most pressure groups use a number of **legal** methods when trying to influence decision makers. The methods a pressure group uses will depend on its relationship with decision makers. If a pressure group feels that it has a strong influence, it will probably be prepared to keep its actions low-key and in fact may work directly with the government while putting its concerns forward. These groups are sometimes referred to as **insider** groups. On the other hand, if a pressure group feels that it is not influential or that decision makers are simply ignoring it, then it may turn against the government by publicly protesting. This will often set it on a collision course with the government. These pressure groups will seek to sway public opinion against the government, and are sometimes referred to as **outsider** pressure groups. The more public a pressure group's methods are, the more likely it is to become an outsider group.

Contacting decision makers

Pressure groups contact their representatives, such as councillors and MPs or MSPs, to make their feelings known and ask for support. In fact there are many representatives who are themselves members of pressure groups. Contact may take the form of a letter, email or even a face-to-face meeting. The power of this method lies in many people contacting their representatives at once. A pressure group may also arrange a meeting with a representative in order to lobby for his or her support. That is, it will ask that councillor, MP or MSP to publicly back a campaign and even try to persuade him or her to vote a certain way over an issue.

Petitions

Pressure groups use public petitions to show decision makers that the public feel strongly about their issue. They also send petitions to large businesses and to the government in order to put pressure on them to change their work practices. One of the most successful petitions was organised by the Snowdrop Campaign, which gained a huge amount of support from the public in its attempt to ban the private ownership of handguns. Over 750,000 people signed the petition in response to the 1996 Dunblane shootings in which 16 children and their teacher were killed.

Marches, demonstrations and rallies

Pressure groups can arrange public protests as long as they give notice to the authorities and conduct them in a legal manner. These protests can take the form of a march along city streets, a demonstration outside an important building, or a rally in a large public space. These can be a very effective way of getting the public's and media's attention and promoting the issue. Outsider pressure groups are far more likely to organise a march than insider groups.

Case study: Stop the War Coalition

In February 2003 the biggest ever single pressure group march took place in London to voice opposition to the proposal to begin military operations in Iraq. Over a million people took to the streets in an event organised by the Stop the War Coalition. Marches also took place in Glasgow and Belfast. Although the event was largely peaceful, four anti-war activists were arrested after more than 20 people held a sit-down protest at Piccadilly Circus. The UK government pressed ahead with its plans.

Figure 4.1 Protestors marched past the Houses of Parliament on their way to a rally in Hyde Park in February 2003.

Poster, leaflet and Internet campaigns

Most pressure groups ask for donations or a membership fee from their followers. This allows them to pay for campaign materials such as posters and leaflets. They then target areas by handing out leaflets in the street or posting them through doors. They also pay expenses for volunteers to approach people in busy city centres to encourage them to sign petitions, join the group or make donations. The larger the pressure group the more finances it will have. Large pressure groups such as Amnesty International create Internet viral campaigns and use social media such as Facebook and Twitter to promote their cause.

Mass media

Some pressure groups make effective use of television, radio and newspapers to promote their cause and put pressure on decision makers. This could be on a small scale, such as appearing in a local newspaper, or it might involve the appearance of a panellist on a national television current affairs programme such as *Question Time*, or as a guest on a news programme. Many also create websites and online campaigns in an effort to appeal to a wide audience.

 Show your understanding

1 Describe, in detail, what is meant by:
   (a) insider pressure groups
   (b) outsider pressure groups.
2 Look at the methods used by pressure groups.
   (a) List them in order of what you feel are the most effective methods.
   (b) For your top two methods, explain why you feel that they are more effective.
   (c) For your last choice, explain why you feel that it may be less effective.

Branch out

3 Working in a group, consider an issue which you all feel strongly about. Imagine you are setting up a pressure group about this issue. Complete the following tasks on a large poster.

   (a) In the middle write the name of your group.
   (b) Explain what your aims are and who you are targeting.
   (c) State whether you will be an insider or outsider group. Explain the advantages and disadvantages of your choice.
   (d) Select which methods you are going to use and for each explain what you hope to achieve using this method.
   (e) Include drawings and illustrations to enhance your poster.

Why are pressure groups allowed to take action?

Pressure groups work on the principle of **free speech**, which is a cornerstone of democracy. They are legally protected as they have a right to express their opinions; however, they must follow certain rights and responsibilities as part of this legal protection. If they do not, they will be committing an illegal act and will be prosecuted.

Rights	Responsibilities
They have the right to protest through marches, demonstrations and industrial action.	They must protest legally by following procedures and ensuring protests are peaceful.
They have the right to promote their cause by using mass media and new media.	They cannot slander individuals or tell lies in order to try to persuade people.
They can actively try to recruit new members.	They must not try to force people to join and they cannot bully or intimidate those who oppose their aims.
They can contact representatives to try to gain their support.	They must not intimidate politicians. They cannot threaten, blackmail or use terrorism to further their cause.
They can organise a petition to show public support.	They cannot falsify signatures; the support must be genuine.

Table 4.2 Rights and responsibilities of pressure groups

Case study: UK pressure groups in action

Mumsnet: Let Girls Be Girls

Mumsnet was set up in January 2000 as a website and forum for parents to give and receive advice. It has grown into the busiest website for parents in the UK and has more than 2 million registered users. This has led to it becoming a very influential pressure group. In the run-up to the 2010 general election all political parties sought the backing of Mumsnet and their potential 2 million voters. In addition, the vast majority of its members are a key group of floating voters (voters who do not vote for the same political party in every election) and are targeted during campaigns. During Mumsnet's 10th anniversary celebrations former prime minister Gordon Brown and his wife Sarah Brown gave keynote speeches. In 2010 Mumsnet launched the **Let Girls Be Girls** campaign, which aimed to curb the sexualisation of children by asking retailers to commit not to sell children's products which play upon, emphasise or exploit their sexuality. Early in 2012 the campaign was extended to tackle 'lads' mags', calling on newsagents and supermarkets not to display them in children's sight. Mumsnet wrote to a number of retailers and arranged several meetings with government officials. As a result the government has published a report recommending a series of rules and procedures for retailers. Education Secretary Michael Gove commented, 'Mumsnet has been loud, clear and effective in its Let Girls Be Girls campaign.'

Figure 4.2 Mumsnet is a pressure group for parents.

Gurkha Justice Campaign

In 2009 after a campaign fronted by actress Joanna Lumley, the Gurkha Justice Campaign finally won its fight for citizenship for former British soldiers. The campaign involved a number of petitions and rallies. The group also successfully lobbied politicians and, through Joanna Lumley, gained the support of the mass media. In 2009 the government suffered an embarrassing defeat in the House of Commons. Gurkhas, who are recruited from Nepal, have been part of the British Army for almost 200 years, but some 36,000 Gurkhas who left before 1997 had been denied UK residency. The prime minister at the time, Gordon Brown, commented, 'I believe it is possible for us to honour our commitments to the Gurkhas and to do so in a way that protects the public finances.'

Figure 4.3 Joanna Lumley fronted the campaign on behalf of the Gurkhas.

Case study: Scottish pressure groups in action

Wind farm protests at the Scottish Parliament

In April 2012, US entrepreneur Donald Trump spoke before the Scottish Parliament's Economy and Energy Committee. Mr Trump was attending as he disagreed with government plans to build an new offshore wind farm off the coast of Aberdeenshire. He was concerned that the project would be visible from his new luxury golf resort on the Menie Estate. Outside the Parliament, opposing pressure groups were demonstrating, two in support of and one in opposition to the wind farm. **Friends of the Earth Scotland** and **Wind Is Good Scotland (WIGS)** staged a peaceful rally in protest at Mr Trump's opposition. The group's leader, Stan Blackley, said, 'We find it rather strange that a US tycoon and reality TV star can come over here, buy land and trash it, then seek to tell us what we should do with our energy and economic future as a nation.' Opposing them, **Communities Against Turbines Scotland (CATS)** staged a 500-person march down the Royal Mile with placards which read 'No to turbines. Protect our coastline'. The event generated a large media presence and public exposure for both causes.

Faslane peace camp

For 30 years there has been an anti-nuclear protest camp outside the gates of Faslane Naval Base, which is situated on the Gare Loch to the north of the River Clyde. The base contains the UK's nuclear Trident submarines. Over the years protestors have attempted to undermine security at the base, including one occasion when three protestors gained entry dressed as Santa Claus. There are six permanent residents who live basic lives in caravans with no fresh water supplies. They do, however, have visitors on a daily basis. Most of the time they protest peacefully and will continue to do so as long as there are nuclear weapons on the Clyde. Scotland's First Minister Alex Salmond has pledged that an independent Scotland would be nuclear free.

Figure 4.5 The logo of the Campaign for Nuclear Disarmament

Figure 4.4 The protest outside the Scottish Parliament in April 2012

Show your understanding

1 Why are pressure groups allowed to take action?
2 Look at Table 4.2 and the case studies on pressure groups in action. For each case study:
   (a) Explain what rights they were using in their campaigns.
   (b) Explain the responsibility that is attached to the right and whether the group followed this.
   (c) Explain the impact of the action taken by the pressure group.

Issues with pressure groups

Do pressure groups threaten democracy?

Law breaking

Some pressure groups flaunt the rules and break the law. Many groups feel that they need to take desperate measures in order to make their voice heard. The consequence of these actions is often tighter controls on protests, demonstrations and marches, and at times criticism of heavy-handed tactics by the police.

G8 summit, Gleneagles

The group **Make Poverty History** organised a series of events and protests in July 2005 as Scotland hosted the G8 summit. The summit is an annual meeting by the leaders of the richest industrialised nations. The group had hoped to persuade the leaders to cancel any debts owed to them by countries from the developing world. Most of the demonstrations were peaceful, but anti-capitalist protestors clashed with police and 750 people were arrested.

Fathers4Justice

Fathers4Justice is an organisation which aims to reform family law and give men equal parental status, especially in situations such as divorce. It has illegally protested in a number of ways including scaling the UK Parliament and other buildings dressed as superheroes. In 2004 the group sparked controversy

when it threw a bag of purple flour over Prime Minister Tony Blair inside the Commons chamber. This was seen as a serious security breach and large glass screens are now in place in the viewing gallery of the House of Commons.

Student riots, London

In 2010 a large student protest in London against a rise in tuition fees in England and Wales ended in violence when 14 police officers were injured, the Christmas tree in Trafalgar Square was set alight, shop windows were smashed, statues in Parliament Square were damaged, and there was damage to Conservative Headquarters during an occupation. Most disturbingly, the car in which Prince Charles and his wife Camilla, Duchess of Cornwall, were travelling was attacked, which triggered a huge security alert. The protest did not force a U-turn by the government and they pressed ahead with their plans. It did, however, greatly raise awareness of the issue by the general public.

UK Uncut

Another example is the group UK Uncut who, in 2011, occupied a London luxury food store, Fortnum & Mason, and staged a sit-in. The group were protesting about the amount of tax the company had paid. During the sit-in, protestors overwhelmed police officers and took control of the store. Over 125 protesters were arrested. Most were later released but ten protestors were charged with aggravated trespass. Fortnum & Mason claimed that lost sales amounted to more than £54,000. UK Uncut is a group which uses new media to organise protests quickly and its actions are under constant surveillance by the police.

Unfair influence

Pressure groups are sometimes accused of having unfair influence on decision making. They put pressure on councillors, MPs and MSPs, yet represent a minority group with a very biased outlook on situations. In addition, some pressure groups are very large and so they can exert more influence than smaller groups. This is seen by many as being unfair, especially when it is considered that many pressure groups are undemocratic and do not shape their policies according to their members' wishes.

Popularity

There is concern that while more and more people are drawn away from representative democracy and political parties, pressure groups are finding that their memberships are increasing every year. There is a belief that traditional politics is outdated and people, especially among the young, find that the alternative offered by pressure groups is much more connected to their way of thinking. This is largely because of the effective use by pressure groups of new media, such as social networks. This potentially threatens democracy as Parliament will become increasingly detached from the general public.

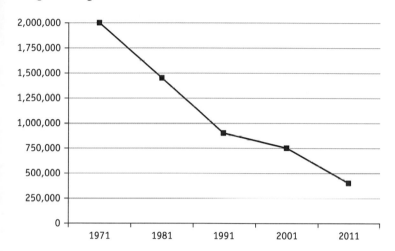

Source: Estimates based on party reports and House of Commons Library.

Figure 4.6 Political party membership, 1971–2011

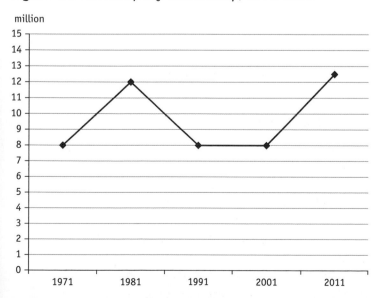

Source: Estimates based on party reports and House of Commons Library.

Figure 4.7 Pressure group membership (including trade unions), 1971–2011

Show your understanding

1   What is the potential consequence of protesting illegally by breaking the law?
2   Look at the examples of law breaking.
    (a) Look at the report on the G8 summit.
        i   Which pressure group was involved in the protest?
        ii What was the effect of protestors breaking the law?
    (b) Look at the report on Fathers4Justice.
        i   What is the aim of Fathers4Justice?
        ii What illegal acts did the group commit and what were the consequences of its actions?
    (c) Look at the report on the student riots.
        i   What were the students protesting over?
        ii What illegal acts were committed?
        iii Do you think these acts helped or hindered the group's cause? Give reasons for your answer.
    (d) Look at the report on UK Uncut.
        i   What is the aim of UK Uncut?
        ii What illegal acts did their members commit?
        iii Explain how the group's use of social media is both a good thing and a bad thing for democracy.
3   'Pressure groups have an unfair influence over democracy in the UK.'
    To what extent do you agree with the above statement? Explain your answer.
4   What is one possible consequence of increased pressure group popularity?
5   In your opinion, what could be done to increase the popularity of party politics?

Develop your skills

6   'Both political parties and pressure groups have seen their popularity decline since 1991 and, in fact, in recent times there has been a sharp fall in pressure group membership.' (*May Allan*)

    Using Figures 4.6 and 4.7, explain why May Allan could be accused of exaggeration.

Trade unions

What you will learn:

1 What a trade union is.
2 What the aims of trade unions are.
3 The methods used by trade unions.
4 Examples of trade union action.
5 Issues with trade unions.

What is a trade union?

Ultimately most employers are in business to make as much profit as possible. Workers represent a cost to them and they will try to make that cost as little as possible. In addition, they also want to get as much productivity as possible out of their workers so that they represent value for money. In contrast, workers want to be suitably rewarded for their hard work. This can bring the two sides into conflict with each other. Workers have found that if they act together collectively they can negotiate a better deal. This is called **collective bargaining**. An employer may be able to ignore an individual worker's concerns but if the workers unite and speak as one, an employer is more likely to listen. Hence, workers form organisations called **trade unions** which negotiate with employers on their behalf.

What are the aims of trade unions?

Almost one worker in every five in the UK is a trade union member – around 7 million workers. People in full-time work spend a large part of their life in their job and, for many people, their job gives them a huge amount of satisfaction. However, many workers also feel that their jobs need to be improved through pay, conditions and benefits. They feel that they are not treated fairly and thus turn to a trade union to help them improve their working conditions. Trade union members tend to be better paid and have better working conditions than those outside unions, as they have someone to stand up for them.

FACT FILE

Issues tackled by trade unions

Trade unions help their members with a large number of issues. Below are some examples:

- pay
- working hours
- redundancy pay
- sexual harassment
- health and safety equipment
- compensation claims
- unfair dismissal appeals.

Almost every improvement in workplace conditions – equal pay laws, stronger health and safety legislation, the National Minimum Wage, better rights for workers – has come about thanks to pressure from trade unions. Trade unions therefore have the following key aims:

- Give advice to members who have a problem at work.
- Represent members in discussions with employers.
- Help improve wages and working conditions.
- Make sure that members' legal rights are enforced at work.
- Make sure that employers provide learning opportunities for members.
- Fight discrimination and help promote equal opportunities at work.
- Provide services for individual members such as medical benefits, legal services, financial services, discounts on insurance, and holidays.
- Lobby the government and others in support of policies and laws that help all people at work.

Show your understanding

1. Explain why there is conflict between workers and employers.
2. Define the term 'collective bargaining'.
3. What percentage of workers are unionised?
4. Why do people join a trade union?

ICT task

Use the Internet to further research workers' rights which are protected by trade unions.

- Go to the following webpage: www.tuc.org.uk/tuc/rights_main.cfm
- Click on the link Basic Rights @ Work.
- List the eight basic rights that workers have.
- Chose three rights and provide a short summary of each of them.

Case study: National Minimum Wage

In 1998 the Labour government introduced the National Minimum Wage Act. This Act established a basic rate of pay of £3.60 per hour for all workers aged 21 and over in 1999. The law requires this amount to increase every year in line with inflation. By 2012 this rate had increased to £6.08 per hour. The National Minimum Wage was introduced largely due to pressure from trade unions. The TUC was concerned about the fall in union membership. These non-unionised workers would not be able to negotiate fair wages through collective bargaining and many found themselves working for very poor wages.

Figure 4.8 The logo of Unison, the UK's largest public service union

How are trade unions managed?

Trade unions are a key part of living in a democracy. While we have laws that protect our personal rights, some workers find themselves being poorly treated by employers. As trade unions are an important part of living in a democracy, they are run on a democratic basis.

National level

At a national level, trade unions often work together to fight for workers' rights. This gives them influence over government and other decision makers. The Trades Union Congress (TUC) is an umbrella organisation under which many trade unions come together. It is able to fight for every worker in the UK.

Individual trade unions

Individually, trade unions try to negotiate the best working conditions for their members and to support their members on any occasion when there is disagreement between workers and employers. At this level trade unions are fully democratic. Within

each workplace, union members elect a **union representative**. These representatives are traditionally known as 'shop stewards', and they help organise members' payments to the union. They have the responsibility to liaise with union members, usually during an arranged meeting, over any issues and concerns that they have. They then present these issues to the employer and seek to have them resolved. In addition, they attend regional and/or national meetings where major policy decisions are made.

Union members also democratically elect members of the union's National Executive Committee and elect its overall leader, known as the general secretary. In many ways this process is exactly the same as electing parliamentary representatives. Selections are made in a secret ballot and the results are open and fair.

UNION REPRESENTATIVE NEEDED

The members of the Workers' Union require a shop steward for the Bergeddie Textile Factory.

Job responsibilities:

- liaising between the union and workers
- organising regular meetings with members
- attending monthly meetings with the factory management to express members' concerns
- promoting the union and recruiting new members
- maintaining the union noticeboard
- advising union members of their rights
- supporting members if action needs to be taken by representing them in meetings.

The successful candidate will have the following qualities:

- good organisational skills
- well respected within the workplace
- confidence to stand up to management
- a good knowledge of working practices and workers' rights
- excellent communication skills
- be a current member of the union and workforce.

If you are interested put your name forward for election!

Please note: this position is voluntary but expenses will be paid by the union.

Show your understanding

1 Why did trade unions support the creation of the National Minimum Wage?
2 Describe, in detail, the role of a shop steward.
3 In what ways are trade unions democratic organisations?
4 Imagine you are a shop steward. Write down the three most important qualities you would need to have and explain why they would be important for the role.

How do trade unions put pressure on employers?

Trade unions have a number of different ways that they can put pressure on employers to give their members the best possible working conditions. Each situation will require a different method of applying pressure and any decisions made will be democratically supported by the members.

FACT FILE

Industrial action

Industrial action means that a union's members change their working practices in order to put pressure on their employer to meet their demands. Union members will be balloted and if the industrial action is agreed upon, it could take the following forms:

Overtime ban – union members refuse to work any hours beyond their contractual agreements. In some workplaces this will have a serious effect on productivity and potential profit for the employer. However, it will also affect the earnings of workers.

Go-slow – union members do not attempt to be highly productive. Together they will agree to take more time to do their job. Again, this will affect productivity and so the employer will be under pressure to give in to demands.

Work-to-rule – union members work only to their contracts and do not take on any extra duties. For example, in a school, all teachers refuse to organise any school trips and lunchtime or after-school clubs.

Strike – seen by many to be the ultimate action by workers. Union members withdraw their labour completely and so do not work. Workers will usually form a picket line outside their workplace to try to persuade other workers to join them on strike. This puts serious pressure on employers but it also results in a loss of earnings for employees. Even the threat of a strike can sometimes be effective in gaining concessions from employers

Show your understanding

1 Explain what is meant by 'industrial action'.
2 Describe, in detail, the meaning and impact of:
   (a) an overtime ban
   (b) a go-slow
   (c) work-to-rule
   (d) a strike.
3 What is the purpose of a picket line?

Figure 4.9 In November 2011 public sector trade unions throughout the UK arranged a one-day strike against changes to pensions, involving more than 2 million workers.

Figure 4.10 The Fire Brigades Union called a strike in 2003 and formed picket lines outside fire stations across the UK. The army had to come in and help provide a fire service.

Rights	Responsibilities
Trade unions have the right to take industrial action.	They must do this legally by following procedures and ensuring protests are peaceful.
They have the right to recruit new members.	They cannot force or bully people into joining.
Trade unions must be consulted about changes to working conditions by employers.	Trade unions must ensure that they act with their members' consent and do not act in their own interests.
Trade unions can ask about changes to pay and working conditions.	They cannot make unreasonable demands or threats.

Table 4.3 Rights and responsibilities of trade unions

Case study: Industrial action in the UK

British Airways cabin crew strike

From 2009 to 2011, British Airways cabin crew who were members of the Unite union went on strike for a total of 22 days. The dispute was about cost-cutting measures such as wage freezes, reductions in cabin crew numbers and the taking away of employee benefits such as reduced flight prices. The industrial action was said to have cost the airline over £150 million in lost revenue. Around 200,000 passengers were affected by the strikes. After almost two years of industrial action and negotiation, the airline agreed to restore the workers' benefits and improve pay scales; however, major cost-cutting to the cabin crew operations did take place.

NHS doctors stage a go-slow

In June 2012, NHS doctors who were members of their union, the British Medical Association (BMA), voted to stage a one-day go-slow in protest against proposed changes to pensions. The BMA said that the industrial action by doctors – their first since 1975 – had successfully shown the depth of anger at changes that will force them to contribute more and work longer for their pensions, and had sent ministers 'a strong message that a fairer approach must be found'. Figures supplied by the NHS showed that 2,703 patients in England had their operation cancelled and another 18,717 were unable to attend their scheduled hospital outpatient appointment. In Scotland 3,650 patients missed out and in Northern Ireland the figure was 897.

Case study: Industrial action in Scotland

Scottish rail staff stage two 24-hour walkouts

The National Union of Rail, Maritime and Transport Workers (RMT) organised a two-day strike in February 2012. This followed a three-day strike during Christmas of the previous year. Bob Crow, general secretary of the RMT, said: 'RMT has tried to reach a negotiated settlement to this unilateral ripping-up of a local arrangement, but unfortunately the management has refused to see sense and has failed to engage with us at all since the strike action over Christmas. RMT members will not stand by while management unilaterally rips up agreements and practices that have been in place at local level for decades.'

The dispute affected 32 staff working at the west of Scotland signalling centre and concerned a practice dating back to the 1970s known as 'slotting in', in which the most senior member of staff was automatically appointed to any vacant position. Network Rail has claimed the slotting-in system is outdated and staff should be appointed on merit.

Scottish high school teachers decide to work to rule

In May 2012, Scottish secondary school teachers who were members of the Scottish Secondary Teachers Association (SSTA) union voted 85% in favour of limiting their work to the 35 hours specified in their contracts. This followed a one-day strike on 30 November 2011 in which teachers of all unions withdrew their labour, causing widespread disruption as many parents had to take the day off to look after their children. The conflict revolved around pay freezes, changes to pensions and changes to working practices in Scotland. The largest teaching union, the Educational Institute of Scotland (EIS), decided not to take any further industrial action and to negotiate with the Scottish government.

Figure 4.11 The majority of Scottish secondary school teachers voted to 'work to rule' in May 2012.

Show your understanding

1 Look at Table 4.3. What guidelines do trade unions need to follow in order to legally take industrial action?
2 Look at the examples of trade union action in the UK and in Scotland.
   (a) Look at the case study on British Airways cabin crew.
      i Why did British Airways staff go on strike?
      ii What impact did the strike have on the company and passengers?
      iii What was the final outcome of the dispute?
   (b) Look at the case study on NHS doctors.
      i Who arranged the doctors' industrial action?
      ii Why were the doctors on a go-slow?
      iii What was the impact of the action?
      iv It was reported that only 20% of doctors took part in the go-slow. Why do you think many doctors would be reluctant to take industrial action?

Show your understanding

(Continued)

(c) Look at the case study on Scottish rail staff.
  i Why do you think the RMT chose the Christmas period to go on strike in 2011?
  ii What was the dispute about?
(d) Look at the case study on Scottish secondary school teachers.
  i Why were members of the SSTA on a work-to-rule?
  ii What other action had teachers taken in the dispute?

  iii List five ways in which you think school life could be changed by a work-to-rule by teachers.

Branch out

3 In groups of four, choose one of the case studies above. One pair should take on the role of general secretary of the union and the other pair the role of chief executive of the company or organisation. Both write a short statement stating your point of view including the potential disruption caused by the industrial action and present this to each other.

What methods do trade unions use?

In most cases trade unions will use negotiation to try to convince management to give the workers better working conditions. This might be over better pay, improving their working environment and any benefits they may get through their employment. This usually takes the form of a series of meetings. If an agreement cannot be reached, the trade union has two options: reduce their demands or ballot their members for **industrial action**.

Issues with trade union membership

Decline

At the height of trade union powers in the 1970s around 80% of workers in the UK were members of a trade union. At that time the UK had strong shipbuilding, steel and coal industries. These primary sector industries were traditionally the home of trade unions. During the 1980s the unions came into conflict with Margaret Thatcher's Conservative government and many of these industries were reduced substantially. Since that time the UK economy has changed dramatically and most UK workers are based in the tertiary or service sectors such as retail and customer services rather than in the primary sector or in manufacturing. As a result there has been a long decline in trade union membership.

Many people would argue that trade unions are not as relevant today as they once were, as they represent a smaller section of the UK workforce. However, they still represent a large section of workers and can still influence decision making at parliamentary level.

FACT FILE

Reasons for the decline of trade union membership

- Better working conditions have resulted in fewer people feeling the need to join a union.
- The decline in UK manufacturing industry has damaged the core base of trade union membership.
- This has been matched by the growth of the service sector, in which only 13% are unionised.
- There has been growth in the number of foreign-owned companies, which are traditionally non-union.
- The number of part-time workers, who may find the membership fee too high, has increased.
- There is a growing number of entrepreneurs, who are self-employed and would have no reason to join a union.
- Fewer young people are in unions, with a third of those over 50 in unions, compared with less than a quarter of those aged 25 to 50.

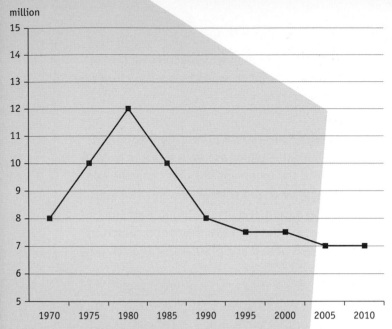

Figure 4.12 Trade union membership in the UK, 1970–2010

Show your understanding

1 Give two reasons for the decline in trade unions.
2 Look at the reasons for the decline of trade unions. For each point:
  (a) give further explanation on why it has impacted on membership
  (b) provide examples to back up your answer.

Develop your skills

3 'Trade union membership has been in decline since 1970.' (*Robyn Jones*)

  Using Figure 4.12, explain why Robyn Jones could be accused of exaggeration.

The influence of the media
What is the media?

Media or **mass media** is a general term used to describe the various ways information and the news are communicated to the public.

In terms of the media's influence on politics we will study the following:

- newspapers
- television
- the Internet.

These forms of media can be categorised into different types. Newspapers are referred to as 'print media', television is known as 'broadcast media' and the Internet is branded as 'electronic media'. In recent years, advancements in electronic media have meant that the Internet is becoming increasingly significant in politics in Scotland and the UK.

What is the role of the media?

The media has various roles in society depending on its form. Art, film and music, although often carrying a message, are primarily produced to **entertain** us. Likewise, television has many roles: there are various genres of entertainment programmes, such as soaps and reality television, as

What you will learn:

1 Definition and role of the media.
2 The influence of the media on people and politics in Scotland and the UK.
3 Who controls the media.
4 Who owns the media.

well as documentaries, news and current affairs programmes to **educate** and **inform**. Buying a newspaper or watching television provides us with a source of information that informs and educates us about local, national and international events. Indeed, newspapers and news channels also have websites that many people are now using instead of buying a print copy of a newspaper or watching the news on TV in the evening. The rise of electronic media, or **new media**, is allowing people to access information instantly. Smartphones let people read about politics and current affairs in seconds by reading newspaper apps, watching the news or listening to the radio, all on their handset. Furthermore, **social media** is carving an important role in the media world with over a billion people accessing sites like Facebook and Twitter on a daily basis.

Show your understanding

1 What is 'mass media'?
2 What various forms can the media take?
3 'The media's role is simply to entertain us.' Provide evidence to oppose this statement.
4 Describe 'social media' and its importance.

What is the influence of the media?

There is little doubt that the vast majority of information that the public consumes about politics and current affairs comes from the media. It is the media that essentially decides what information the public learns and therefore the media plays a huge role in shaping our attitudes and opinions. As we live in a democracy in the UK, we have a **free press** that is allowed to criticise the government and hold it to account over its actions. The work of the media in this role is of obvious significance to politicians, and political parties work hard to ensure the media is favourable to them.

> **Free press:** media that is not restricted or censored by the government.

Newspapers

You will notice when you walk into your local newsagent that there are many different newspapers available to buy. Generally, newspapers can be split into two categories, known as 'tabloids' (popular) and 'broadsheets' (quality). The *Sun* and the *Daily*

Figure 4.13 Newspapers available in Scotland

Record are examples of tabloids, and the *Guardian* and the *Scotsman* are examples of broadsheets.

Every day in the UK over 12 million people buy and read newspapers, with tabloid newspapers far outselling broadsheets. Most newspapers tend to support a particular political party and are biased in favour of them. This means they write positive stories about the party and their leader. It also means they write negative stories about other political parties and present them in a less favourable light. Newspapers are therefore very influential in politics and can persuade people to vote for political parties at election time.

Can newspapers influence elections?

Looking back to the 1992 UK general election, some would argue that newspapers were a factor in deciding the election. The *Sun* (Britain's largest-selling daily newspaper) threw its backing behind the Conservative party and when the Conservatives won, the *Sun* printed the headline 'It's the Sun wot won it'. Newspapers' influence can also be studied by looking at the 2010 UK general election and 2011 Scottish parliament election.

	Tabloids	Broadsheets
Size	Small	Large or compact
Stories	Human interest, celebrity, gossip, sport	Politics, economics, world affairs
Language	Simplistic with lots of photos	More complex with few photos
Headlines	Short	Long and informative
Influence	Biased	Less biased

Table 4.4 Features of tabloid and broadsheet newspapers

Case study: Influence of newspapers on the 2010 UK general election

In the run-up to the 2010 UK general election, public support for the Labour government was declining. Prime Minister Gordon Brown was an unpopular figure and confidence in his leadership was low.

Many newspapers lost faith in Labour and after backing the party for many years decided to shift their support to another party. The *Sun* changed its support from Labour to the Conservatives. The newspaper had decided that, after supporting Labour from 1997 until 2009, the party had 'lost it'.

Other national newspapers also changed support. *The Times* moved from Labour to supporting the Conservatives and the *Guardian* shifted support to the Liberal Democrats. Only a few national newspapers continued to support Labour.

The election result saw the Conservatives returning to power, and the support of national newspapers certainly helped. However, the Conservatives failed to win a crucial overall majority and so the influence of newspapers should not be exaggerated.

Figure 4.14 The front pages of the *Sun* in 1997 and 2009

Case study: Influence of newspapers on the 2011 Scottish Parliament election

In Scotland, the 2011 Scottish Parliament election highlighted the influence of newspapers on politics.

Since the SNP gained power and formed a minority government in 2007 without the full support of any Scottish national newspaper, it could be argued that newspapers have little influence over politics. However, in 2011 the SNP managed to do even better – it won by such a distance that it was able to form a majority government.

In the lead-up to the 2011 Scottish Parliament election, the *Scottish Sun* backed the SNP for the first time, after opposing it in previous elections. SNP Leader Alex Salmond was delighted with the support and felt it would help the party gain more voters. The election result saw the SNP win the

election and go on to form the first majority government in Scottish parliamentary history.

It is difficult to assess if the SNP would still have won by such a margin without the *Sun*'s support, but it is fair to say that the *Sun*'s backing did little harm to the SNP's chances in 2011.

Figure 4.15 The *Scottish Sun* backed the SNP in 2011.

Newspaper	Circulation in 2007	Circulation in 2012
Sun	3.2 million	2.5 million
Daily Mail	2.3 million	1.9 million
Daily Mirror	1.6 million	1.1 million
Daily Record	418,000	290,000
Guardian	384,000	215,000

Table 4.5 Newspaper circulation rates 2007 and 2012

Is the influence of newspapers declining?

With the rise of electronic media the influence of newspapers on politics is in slight decline. The number of print newspapers sold on a daily basis is decreasing as the way people access the news is changing. On smartphones people can buy a newspaper app for a one-off payment and have constant access to that paper's news. People can also access the Internet and view newspapers' websites (which provide up-to-the-minute stories) free of charge. Newspapers are still popular and they still have an influence on politics. However, in the not so distant future their influence will mainly be felt through electronic means rather than in print.

The phone-hacking activities of Rupert Murdoch's *News of the World* and its closure have weakened the influence of the Murdoch empire (see Chapter 2, page 33).

Television

As a form of broadcast media, television has strict guidelines to follow regarding what is broadcast. Unlike newspapers, television has to be **politically impartial** and cannot support a particular political party or agenda. Television channels are regulated by an independent body called Ofcom to make sure they are not biased in their reporting. For example, at election time each of the major parties in the UK will be allowed an equal amount of time for party political broadcasts. This prevents any party gaining an advantage and allows the public to learn about each party in a fair manner.

 Show your understanding

1 What does 'free press' mean?
2 Describe the difference between tabloids and broadsheets.
3 What does it mean to say a newspaper is biased in favour of a political party?
4 Look at the case study on the influence of newspapers on the 2010 UK general election.
   (a) Why did many papers decide to shift support away from Labour?
   (b) Which papers supported the Conservatives?
   (c) Who eventually won the 2010 UK election?
5 Look at the case study on the influence of newspapers on the 2011 Scottish Parliament election.
   (a) Why was Alex Salmond 'delighted' with the *Sun*'s support?
   (b) Why could the result be said to have been 'historic'?
6 Explain, in detail, why the influence of newspapers is declining.

Branch out

7 Can you list 10 newspapers that are available in the UK? Include local or regional papers as well.

Develop your skills

8 'The circulation of newspapers in Britain has decreased from 2007 to 2012. However, the circulation of the *Daily Mirror* rose by half a million in the same period.' *(Hannah Masson)*

Using Table 4.5, explain to what extent Hannah Masson can be accused of exaggeration.

Figure 4.16 The 2010 leaders' debate

Can television influence elections?

The influence of television was fairly limited until 2010, when the first ever televised leaders' debates took place: in the lead-up to the 2010 UK general election, the leaders of the three main political parties took part in debates shown on television. The debates ended up having a massive influence on the election campaign of each party: the Liberal Democrat leader, Nick Clegg, came across exceptionally well on television. In comparison, Conservative Leader David Cameron and then Labour Prime Minister Gordon Brown failed to impress in front of the cameras. After the debates, it seemed that support among the public for the Liberal Democrats had increased dramatically but in the end the result of the 2010 election was a disappointment for the party.

Televised leaders' debates also took place before the 2011 Scottish Parliament election. Unlike the UK leaders' debates a year earlier, there was no major impact on public opinion towards the leaders of the main parties. If the debates benefited any party it was the SNP, with Alex Salmond coming across as assured on television while then Labour Leader Iain Gray seemed nervous and tense.

New media and the Internet

Over recent years the Internet has become increasingly popular. It is estimated that over 70% of the UK population access the Internet on a daily basis. This is done not only through computers but now also through mobile phones and tablet devices. The Internet provides a portal for political parties to utilise various platforms to connect with the public. Almost all political parties have websites and many now have Facebook pages, Twitter feeds, blogs and even YouTube channels that aim to win the support of the general public. Political parties are finding social media particularly useful in engaging young people in politics. Indeed, it is much easier and cheaper to follow politicians on Twitter than to buy and read a newspaper every day.

Many individual MPs and MSPs are also engaging with the public through social media. SNP Leader Alex Salmond can boast of having over 25,000 followers on Twitter and Prime Minister David Cameron over 2 million. Such sites allow politicians to communicate directly with the public and the media, as well as to publicise the positive work of their party.

Can new media influence elections?

Both the recent UK and Scottish elections were primarily influenced by newspapers and television. However, the Internet did play a role, with all parties conducting online campaigns. As the next elections come around, the influence new media commands will undoubtedly increase.

Can social media have a negative effect on politics?

With social media being a relatively new phenomenon, MPs and MSPs who regularly use it are essentially 'trail-blazers' and are finding out for themselves the positives and negatives. There are undoubted benefits, such as the ability to connect directly with the public and to present yourself in a positive way. However, a few politicians have already been 'stung' by not using social media carefully.

MP blasted over Olympic opening ceremony tweet

A Conservative MP has attacked the opening ceremony of the 2012 London Olympic Games, branding it 'multicultural rubbish'. While others were lavishing praise on Danny Boyle's £27 million extravaganza, Aidan Burley MP appeared to disagree. The controversial tweet not only could be taken as racist but is rather strange, given the fact that the Mayor of London is also a Conservative party member and is partly responsible for the ceremony.

Aidan Burley faced a backlash from Twitter users, including celebrities such as X Factor host Dermot O'Leary. Burley's boss, Prime Minister David Cameron, stated, 'I think what he said was completely wrong. It was an idiotic thing to say.'

The saga will not help Aidan Burley's career and his future in the Conservative party may be limited.

Show your understanding

1 'Television channels are allowed to support political parties if they choose.' Provide evidence to oppose this statement.
2 Why were the television debates so beneficial for the Liberal Democrats during the 2010 UK election campaign?
3 What impact did television debates have in Scotland in 2011?
4 What percentage of the UK population access the Internet on a daily basis?
5 How do political parties use the Internet to win the support of the public?
6 Why is it important for politicians to be careful when using social media? Refer to the newspaper article 'MP blasted over Olympic opening ceremony tweet'.
7 'Political parties shouldn't bother with new media and should focus on traditional newspapers.' Do you agree or disagree with this statement? Justify your answer.

ICT task

Working in pairs, research how a political party of your choice uses the Internet to connect with the public. Create a 3–5 slide presentation to report back to your class. Include information on the following:

- Does the party have an official website? What does it tell you?
- Does the party use social media? If so, what sites? How many likes/followers?
- Does the party use video sites such as YouTube? How many subscribers?

Added value

Research the influence of the three main forms of media on either the 2010 UK general election or the 2011 Scottish Parliament election. You could present your findings in the form of an online blog or podcast or even create a film with Movie Maker.

Who controls the media?

Although we have a free press in the UK, newspapers have to be controlled and work within the law. The Press Complaints Commission operates a **code of practice** that ensures the press (newspapers and magazines) has a duty to maintain the highest professional standards. This mainly means that newspapers have to take care not to publish inaccurate or misleading information about individuals, groups, companies or political parties. For example, while newspapers are free to be biased towards a political party they must not tell lies or create false news to the detriment of another political party.

Many individuals have sued newspapers for telling lies about them. This is often referred to as suing for 'libel' or 'defamation of character'. Celebrities such as David Beckham and Gordon Ramsay have received substantial payouts in damages from newspapers in recent years.

Who owns the media?

Until the early 1990s, British television was dominated by the terrestrial channels of the British Broadcasting Corporation (BBC) and Independent Television (ITV). The emergence of satellite and cable television has challenged their monopoly of news delivery.

The BBC is owned by the UK public as it is funded by a licence fee that is charged to anyone who owns a television set. On the other hand, Britain's largest satellite broadcaster, BSkyB, is owned by various shareholders with Rupert Murdoch owning a large share, at 39%. His company, News Corporation, also owns Britain's biggest-selling daily newspaper, the *Sun*, as well as *The Times*. The fact that Rupert Murdoch has such a significant stake in the UK media means that he is a very influential person when it comes to politics. For example, he can decide which political party his popular newspapers support from one election to the next. Many people argue that no one person should have such influence, and private media ownership should be limited.

Show your understanding

1 Describe the role of the Press Complaints Commission.
2 Who owns the BBC?
3 What newspapers does Rupert Murdoch own?

Develop your skills

4 'Rupert Murdoch has little influence over UK politics.' (*Luke McCarthy*)

Do you agree or disagree with Luke McCarthy? Give reasons for your answer.

Chapter 5

Assessment: National 4 & 5 Skills and Knowledge

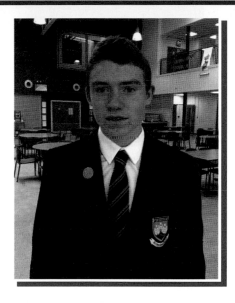

Welcome to National 4 and National 5 Skills and Knowledge!

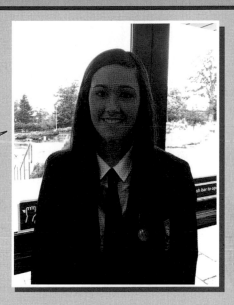

You should now have the skills and knowledge to complete the assessment demands of the Democracy in Scotland and the UK unit of the Modern Studies course. The skills and knowledge required for National 4 and National 5 level are very similar, with National 5 requiring you to handle more detailed sources and to provide greater detail in your knowledge answers.

National 4 Assessment

The National 4 award for Modern Studies is assessed by your teacher and not graded by an external marker. To achieve the award, you need to pass the internal assessment for each of the following units:

- Democracy in Scotland and the United Kingdom
- Social Issues in the United Kingdom
- International Issues
- National 4 Added Value assignment

National 5 Assessment

The National 5 award is made up of both internally and externally marked assessments. To achieve the award, you need to pass the internal assessment for each of the following units:

- Democracy in Scotland and the United Kingdom
- Social Issues in the United Kingdom
- International Issues

The added value unit for National 5 is an externally marked assessment. This consists of two parts:

- National 5 question paper
- National 5 assignment

In Modern Studies we look at a range of issues that affect everyone's lives. These issues are based on evidence gathered through research carried out by a range of different people and organisations, from governments to charities. As part of your qualification you will be expected to carry out a piece of personal research on a particular topic which is relevant to what you have studied. This is called the **Added Value unit assignment** at National 4 and the **assignment** at National 5.

How do I carry out a piece of research?

When researching a topic in Modern Studies, it is important to consider where you will get your information from. In the 21st century you have access to huge amounts of information, most of it at your fingertips on the Internet. However, you need to be conscious of its accuracy and its likelihood of containing bias.

Where do I gather information from?

The information gathered from research can be broken down into two parts: primary information and secondary information.

Primary information

Primary information is evidence that you have gathered by yourself and is unique to your personal research. Your personal research should contain at least two pieces of information gathered by primary research, as well as information gathered from other sources. The ways in which you gather primary evidence can vary greatly – some examples are below.

- Surveys / questionnaires
- Interviews
- Emails
- Letters
- Focus groups
- Field studies

Secondary information

Secondary information is evidence that you have gathered from research that was carried out by others. You should use it to help support your personal research. There are vast amounts of secondary information available, in many different formats – below are just a few examples.

- Newspapers, magazines and books
- Internet search engines and websites
- Television and radio programmes
- Mobile phone apps
- Social media such as Twitter
- Library books and articles

How do I plan my research?

In order to carry out a successful piece of personal research you need to plan it effectively. You will need to keep all evidence of your planning so that your work can be accurately marked.

Topic / Issue

You should agree on a topic to research with your teacher. It must relate to one or more of the issues that you have studied in your course, so it is a good idea to pick something from one of the three units you have studied:

- Democracy in Scotland and the United Kingdom
- Social Issues in the United Kingdom
- International Issues

Hypothesis

If you are being presented at National 5 and you have decided on your topic/issue, then you will have to state a hypothesis which you will revisit in your conclusion. A hypothesis is simply a statement that your personal research will try to prove or disprove.

Sources of information

You may wish to consider the following questions about your primary and secondary sources.

- What useful information have I got from this source to help me research my issue?
- How did I collect this information or where did it come from?
- How reliable is the information gathered from the source?
- Could the source contain bias or exaggeration?

Background knowledge

What relevant knowledge do you have from your Modern Studies course which will help you to research your issue?

Conclusions

Using all of the information gathered, what are your final thoughts on your issue?

Presentation

How are you going to present your sources and findings?

You could choose from the following methods of presenting your Added Value assignment:

- **Oral presentation** – you may want to give a 5 minute talk to the class. This talk should be well organised and can be supported with other materials such as a PowerPoint or Prezi. You could include a question and answer session at the end of your presentation.

- **Written report** – you may wish to submit a structured essay/report or mock newspaper article. You could also create an online blog or wiki to present your findings.

- **Display** – you could create a large and well-structured poster incorporating your findings. After presenting it to the class you could hold a question and answer session.

- **Audio recording** – you could create a scripted podcast to present your findings. The podcast could include interviews or could take the form of a radio broadcast.

- **Video recording** – you may want to create a video recording to help present your findings. You could create a mock news broadcast or a short film and even use software such as iMovie and Movie Maker to aid your presentation.

Sample plan

Below is an example of how a piece of personal research could be planned and structured. You should work with your teacher to consider how you should plan, carry out and present your own piece of research.

Poster Presentation

Area of course: Democracy in Scotland and the United Kingdom

Topic / Issue: Voting age in the UK

Hypothesis: *The majority of people agree that the voting age in the UK should be reduced to 16.*

Introduction: In this section I will explain why I chose the topic and how I collected my information.

Display: In my poster I will include 4 sources of information – the results of a survey/questionnaire, the transcript of an interview with a focus group, a section on secondary sources I used and, lastly, a section on my own knowledge.

Source 1 – Survey / Questionnaire:

I am going to ask my friends, neighbours and family to respond to the following questionnaire. From the questionnaire I will create a bar graph of responses to the key question. I will then give some of the reasons for people's responses and discuss whether the findings of the questionnaire agree or disagree with my hypothesis. Using the questionnaire, I could also gather evidence of which gender or age group is in favour of or against a change in the voting age.

This is what my survey may look like:

Gender			Male		Female	
Age	12–17	18–24	25–40	41–60	60+	
Do you think that the voting age should be reduced to 16?			Yes	No	Undecided	
Give one reason for your answer						

This is what my graph may look like:

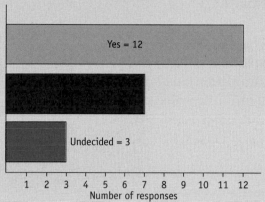

Source 2 – Interview with a focus group:

Using my mobile phone, I will record a discussion session with a focus group of 5 of my classmates. I will ask the following question:

What do you feel are the arguments for and against reducing the voting age to 16?

I will then type up a transcript of the discussion to display on my poster and I will highlight any arguments which agree or disagree with my hypothesis.

My transcript may look like this:

Me: What do you feel are the arguments for and against reducing the voting age to 16?

Person 1: I think that young people are affected by the decisions made by government so they should get the vote.

Person 2: I disagree, most young people do not know enough about politics to make a sensible decision.

Person 3: But giving them the vote would mean politicians would have to start taking an interest in young people.

Person 2: That's true, but I still think that most young people would base their vote on personality rather than who is the best person for the job...

Source 3 – Secondary Sources:

In this section of my poster I will include a newspaper article about the topic that I have found and also evidence from the Electoral Reform Society website. I will make sure to acknowledge the sources of these pieces of information.

Source 4 – My own knowledge:

The final source section of my poster will be based on my own knowledge of the topic. I will organise this into arguments which agree or disagree with my hypothesis.

Research methods: For each source I will consider its relevance, accuracy and whether it could contain bias.

Conclusion: At the bottom of my poster I will present my conclusion, which will consider whether my hypothesis of *The majority of people agree that the voting age in the UK should be reduced to 16* has been proved or disproved.

National 4 Democracy in Scotland and the UK

Assessment Items

At National 4 you will be expected to answer a skills-based question/activity and knowledge and understanding questions/activities. For the internal assessment of this political unit, the skills and knowledge which will be assessed are outlined in outcomes 1 and 2 below.

Outcome 1

- Ability to use a limited range of information to detect and explain bias and exaggeration relating to political issues in Scotland and the United Kingdom

Outcome 2

- Straightforward description and brief explanations demonstrating knowledge and understanding of political issues in Scotland and the United Kingdom

Assessment Evidence

Evidence for successful completion of both outcomes can be based on a range of activities:

- responses to questions
- a presentation
- information posters, or
- participation in group tasks.

The examples which follow are based on written responses.

National 4 Democracy in Scotland

Outcome 1: Skills Question

Study sources 1, 2 and 3 below, then answer the question that follows.

Source 1

Elections for the Scottish Parliament
Number of MSPs Elected

Party	2007 (seats)	2011 (seats)
Scottish National Party (SNP)	47	69
Labour	46	37
Conservatives	17	15
Liberal Democrats	16	5
Green Party	2	2
Others	1	1
Total	**129**	**129**

(N4)

Source 2

Forming the Scottish government 2011

From 2007 until 2011 Scotland was governed by an SNP minority government. After the May 2011 Scottish General Election the SNP won the majority of seats in the Scottish Parliament. The SNP are now the first majority party in the Scottish Parliament and have had greater success in passing new laws.

Source 3

Statements about Scottish politics

- The SNP have had limited success in passing new laws in the Scottish Parliament.

- From 2007 to 2011 Scotland was governed by a minority government.

- The Green Party saw an increase in the number of seats they won in 2011.

- The SNP saw an increase in the number of seats they won in 2011.

Give **two** examples of **exaggeration** from the statements about Scottish politics (Sources 3).

For **each** example, give **one** reason to explain why it is exaggerated.

Your answer must be based only on the information in the sources. **(4 marks)**

Outcome 2: Knowledge and Understanding Question

The Scottish Parliament is responsible for devolved matters in Scotland.

Some people believe that local councillors should be employed full-time as councillors.

(a) Describe **two** devolved matters that are the responsibility of the Scottish Parliament. **(4 marks)**

(b) Give **two** reasons why local councillors should be employed full-time. **(4 marks)**

National 4 Democracy in the UK

Outcome 1: Skills Question

Study sources 1–3 below, then answer the question that follows.

Source 1

Sales of selected British newspapers

Newspaper	Sales figures	
	2001	2011
The Sun	3,288,000	2,904,000
Daily Mirror	2,056,000	1,282,000
Guardian	361,000	276,000
The Times	667,000	480,000
Daily Express	929,000	642,000

Source 2

Political party support in the 2005 and 2010 general elections: selected newspapers

Newspaper	2005	2010
The Sun	Labour	Conservative
Daily Mirror	Labour	Labour
Daily Mail	Conservative	Conservative
Guardian	Labour	Liberal Democrat
The Times	Labour	Conservative
Daily Express	Conservative	Conservative

Source 3

Statements by Claire Willis

- The sales of all newspapers have declined since 2001.
- The *Daily Mirror* has always supported Labour.
- *The Times* has always supported the Conservatives.
- The *Daily Express* has the lowest sales figures.

Give **two** examples of **exaggeration** from the statements about sales of newspapers and political party support made in Source 3.

For **each** example, give **one** reason to explain why it is exaggerated.

Your answer must be based only on the information above.   **(4 marks)**

Outcome 2: Knowledge and Understanding Question

The Prime Minister is the most important person in the Cabinet.

Party workers can help their candidate during a general election campaign.

(a) Describe **two** powers of the Prime Minster.   **(4 marks)**

(b) Give **two** ways in which supporters can help a candidate during a general election campaign.   **(4 marks)**

National 4 Added Value Unit
The Assignment

The Added Value unit will be internally marked by your teacher. The SQA's unit specification document states that in order to pass the Assignment you must research and use information relating to a Modern Studies topic or issue by:

- **Choosing, with support, an appropriate Modern Studies topic** or issue. You should choose an issue that you are interested from any part of the course. Below are some examples from the political unit:

  - Should the voting age be reduced to 16 for all elections?
  - Should Scotland become independent?
  - Should positive discrimination be introduced to improve women's representation in the Scottish or UK Parliament?

- (N4) **Collecting relevant evidence** from at least two different sources. The section on research methods (see pages 128–129) provides useful information on the types of sources that can be used.

- **Organising and using information** collected to address the topic or issue. You should use your skills to decide if the information is balanced or biased and based on fact rather than opinion.

- **Using the knowledge and understanding** you now have to describe and explain the key learning points you wish to make.

- **Applying your Modern Studies skills** in detecting bias or exaggeration, making decisions and drawing conclusions.

- **Presenting your findings and conclusion** on the issue you have chosen. You can present your findings in a variety of ways: as a written piece of research, or a poster, or a talk followed by questions, or you can use digital media such as a blog or journal.

National 4 Added Value Checklist

Name	
Title	

Unit(s)	Democracy in Scotland and the United Kingdom	Social Issues in the United Kingdom	International Issues
Relevant sources of information			
Number and type			
Evidence evaluated			
Skills used			
Detecting bias and exaggeration			
Making decisions			
Drawing conclusions			
Type of presentation			
Written report			
PowerPoint			
Wall display/Other			
Conclusion/Findings			
Based on evidence			
Evidence of individual work (if task is a group/paired activity)			

N4

National 5 Democracy in Scotland and the UK

Assessment Items

At National 5 you will be expected to answer a skills-based question/ activity and knowledge and understanding questions/activities. For the internal assessment of this political unit, the skills and knowledge which will be assessed are outlined in outcomes 1 and 2 below.

Outcome 1

- Ability to use a range of information to detect and explain exaggeration and selective use of facts relating to political issues in Scotland and the United Kingdom

Outcome 2

- Detailed description and explanations demonstrating knowledge and understanding of political issues in Scotland and the United Kingdom

Assessment Evidence

Evidence for successful completion of both outcomes can be based on a range of activities:

- responses to questions
- a presentation
- information posters, or
- participation in group tasks.

The examples which follow are based on written responses.

National 5 Democracy in Scotland

Skills Question

Study Sources 1–3 below, then answer the question that follows.

Source 1

Representation in the Scottish Parliament 1999–2011

Now over a decade since devolution, representation of ethnic minorities and women in the Scottish Parliament is still a controversial issue in Scottish politics. Many people believe that there should be a larger proportion of both ethnic minorities and women in the Parliament to allow for fairer debate.

The number of ethnic minority candidates elected to the Scottish Parliament has increased since 1999. The first two terms saw zero ethnic minority candidates elected with 1 elected in 2007 and 2 elected in 2011 – the highest number yet. However, this still leaves ethnic minorities underrepresented as they make up around 3% of the total Scottish population and only 1.6% of the Scottish Parliament.

Female representation appears slightly healthier with over 30% of MSPs during 1999–2011 being women. In 2003 a record number of 48 female MSPs were elected, but this figure decreased to 45 by 2011. For fair and equal representation, women should always make up around half of elected MSPs as they make up 49% of the Scottish population. This means that 64 MSPs should be female from the total of 129 MSPs that are elected.

Source 2

Representation of ethnic minorities in the Scottish Parliament

Election year	Ethnic population of Scotland	Number of ethnic minority MSPs	As % of MSPs
1999	2%	0	0%
2003	2.2%	0	0%
2007	2.7%	1	0.8%
2011	3%	2	1.6%

Source 3

Representation of women in the Scottish Parliament

Election year	Population of Scotland	Male MSPs (/129)	As% of MSPs	Female MSPs (/129)	As% of MSPs
1999	51% Male 49% Female	81	64%	48	36%
2003	51% Male 49% Female	78	61%	51	39.5%
2007	51% Male 49% Female	86	66.9%	43	33.3%
2011	51% Male 49% Female	84	65.1%	45	34.9%

> *Ethnic minorities and women are poorly represented in the Scottish Parliament but both have seen their representation increase between 1999 and 2011.*
>
> Kevin McNally

Using Sources 1–3, explain why the view of Kevin McNally is selective in its use of facts.

In your answer you should:

- show information that Kevin McNally has selected to support his view

(N5)
- show information that Kevin McNally has **not** selected as it does **not** support his view.

Your answer must be based on all three sources. **(8 marks)**

Knowledge and Understanding Question

> The Scottish Parliament can make decisions about devolved matters for Scotland.

(a) Describe, **in detail**, the devolved matters which the Scottish Parliament can make decisions about for Scotland. **(6 marks)**

> Pressure groups in Scotland use a variety of methods to try and achieve their aims.

(b) Explain, **in detail**, the reasons why pressure groups in Scotland use a variety of methods to try to 'achieve their aims'. **(6 marks)**

National 5 Democracy in the UK

Skills Question

Source 1

UK General Election result 2010

Party	Seats	Change since previous election	Votes (%)	Seats (%)
Conservative	307	+97	36.1	47.2
Labour	258	−91	29.0	38.7
Liberal Democrats	57	−5	23.0	8.9

Source 3

Summary of results

Five million fewer people voted for Labour compared to the 1997 Labour landslide victory.

The number of ethnic minority MPs increased from 14 to 27.

The Conservatives failed once again to make progress in Scotland. They remained the fourth place party with only one MP.

The Green Party elected their first MP, Caroline Luca.

All three sitting 'independent' MPs were defeated.

Source 2

General Election results 2010 by area, UK parties (Great Britain)

England			
Party	Seats	Change since previous election	Votes (%)
Conservative	298	+92	39.5
Labour	191	−87	28.1
Liberal Democrats	43	−4	24.2

Scotland			
Party	Seats	Change since previous election	Votes (%)
Conservative	1	–	16.7
Labour	41	–	42.0
Liberal Democrats	11	–	18.9
SNP	6	–	19.9

Wales			
Party	Seats	Change since previous election	Votes (%)
Conservative	8	+5	26.1
Labour	26	−4	36.3
Liberal Democrats	3	−1	20.1
Plaid Cymru	3	+1	11.3

> *The Conservatives, followed by the Liberal Democrats, were the most successful party in the 2010 General Election across all of the UK and once again the FPTP electoral system ensured no representation from the minority parties or an increase in ethnic minority MPs.*
>
> Michelle Elliot

Using Sources 1–3, explain why the view of Michelle Elliot is selective in its use of facts.

In your answer you should:

- show information that Michelle Elliot has selected to support her view
- show information that Michelle Elliot has **not** selected as it does **not** support her view.

Your answer must be based on all three sources. **(8 marks)**

Knowledge and Understanding Question

> The Prime Minister is the most powerful member of the Cabinet.

(a) Describe, **in detail**, the powers of the Prime Minster. **(6 marks)**

> The British public supports changes to the House of Lords.

(b) Explain, **in detail**, why the British public supports changes to the House of Lords. **(6 marks)**

National 5 Course Assessment

Added Value is assessed in the course assessment and is made up of two components:

- a question paper with activities from each of the three units
- the National 5 Assignment.

Course Assessment Structure

Component 1 – Question paper

The question paper is worth a total of 60 marks, with 20 marks for each unit of the course. Overall 26 marks are for skills and 34 marks are for knowledge and understanding.

Component 2 – Assignment

The assignment is worth a total of 20 marks. Of these 14 marks are for skills and 6 marks are for knowledge and understanding.

Total marks available   80 marks

To gain the course award all units and course assessments must be passed. The marks you achieve in the question paper and assignment are added together and an overall mark will indicate a pass or fail. From this, your course award will then be graded.

National 5 Assignment

The National 5 Assignment is a personal research activity which must include at least two methods of collecting information with comment on the effectiveness of the methods used. The information collected should display knowledge and understanding of the topic or issue chosen. The results of your research will be written up under controlled examination conditions. As previously mentioned, 20 marks are given to the Assignment.

Preparation for the Assignment

1 Research question

You should choose an appropriate topic or issue, for example, *Voting age in all elections and referenda in Scotland should be reduced to 16* (see page 135 for examples of other topics). You may choose an issue from any of the three individual units or you may choose a topic that integrates two units of the course, for example, *The democracies in Scotland and South Africa have similarities and differences*. The best practice is to present the research question in the form of a hypothesis with a clear aim.

2 Research methods

As part of your assignment, you must gather relevant evidence to support your hypothesis using at least two methods of collecting information. There are a range of methods you could use, including field work, referencing books or the Internet. You are expected to evaluate the strengths and weaknesses of each research method you use and to analyse your findings. Remember that two methods are the minimum you are required to use and you might wish to widen your range to more than two.

3 Research findings

This is the section which will display your detailed knowledge and understanding in describing and explaining issues relevant to your hypothesis, including the identification of a variety of viewpoints. Here you must also evaluate the evidence you have gathered and describe what it shows.

4 Research conclusions

Once you have successfully analysed and explained the information you have gathered, you should make conclusions based on your research. Your conclusions must be relevant to your research issue and link back to your original hypothesis. Try to avoid simply repeating the findings you have previously given.